Needlepoint

Cathay Books

Needlepoint
The art of canvas embroidery
by Mary Rhodes

Contents

Introduction

This book is about that form of embroidery which has been variously known as canvas work, canvas embroidery, petit-point, canvas needlework, tapestry work and needlepoint.

The most suitable of the many names applied to this work are undoubtedly canvas work or canvas embroidery. The old name of tapestry work is not acceptable today, because it should be used to designate only hand-woven tapestry which has a warp and weft of its own, and not stitchery done upon an existing fabric. Petit-point was a term once used to describe embroidery upon canvas, because most pieces were worked entirely in the stitch known as petit-point or tent stitch.

In the past, the stitches used in canvas work tended to be somewhat limited in number. Designs were often very fine and intricate, thus exercising a restricting influence upon the workers, who inclined towards an almost exclusive use of tent stitch in interpreting them. Modern abstract designs have given a new dimension to canvas work and have allowed the embroiderer to experiment with many types of stitches and particularly to achieve wonderful textural effects by a skilful use of a great variety of square stitches.

Modern canvas work has also gained much from the increased number and variety of threads and colours now available which enable the embroiderer to experiment in the interpretation of designs in many exciting ways.

However, one way in which modern canvas embroidery could perhaps be said to have become more limited than the canvas work of the past is in its practical use. In recent years there has been a tendency to use embroidery almost exclusively for the production of wall-panels and pictures, neglecting very considerably its former uses. This book, it is hoped, will restore the balance by suggesting a number of attractive ways in which canvas work can be used to make personal accessories such as belts, necklets, bracelets, purses and handbags and covers for such objects as jewel cases and table-lamp bases, as well as to produce striking wall-panels.

I have enjoyed writing this book and hope it will bring pleasure to many people, especially to those who have not yet fully experienced how much can be achieved by working with a few shades of wool upon a piece of canvas. Canvas work can be very time-consuming, but it brings a great and absorbing interest to the worker and provides a gratifying reward in itself, when a beautiful piece is completed.

I also hope that readers will try to create something original in canvas work – and by that I do not mean something completely 'way out', or something that has never been seen before, because that is hardly possible. What I do mean is that, instead of buying a traced canvas to work, they should try to develop a design of their own by following some of the suggestions in this book. Do not be

6

page 1:
Blue and silver pearl pendant

pages 2–3:
Seashore

page 4:
A detail of the Bradford Table Carpet. Worked with wool and silk entirely in tent stitch on a linen canvas, the carpet measures 13 by $5\frac{3}{4}$ feet. The border shows a representative Elizabethan scene and the centre panel is of a trellis covered with vines and grapes.

'Golden Wing'. This very lovely panel is worked on 16 mesh canvas mainly in smyrna and tent stitches on a background of mosaic stitch. Large topaz and amethyst jewels, thick and thin gold cords and orion cloth, together with silk and wool, combine to produce a rich textural effect. ▷

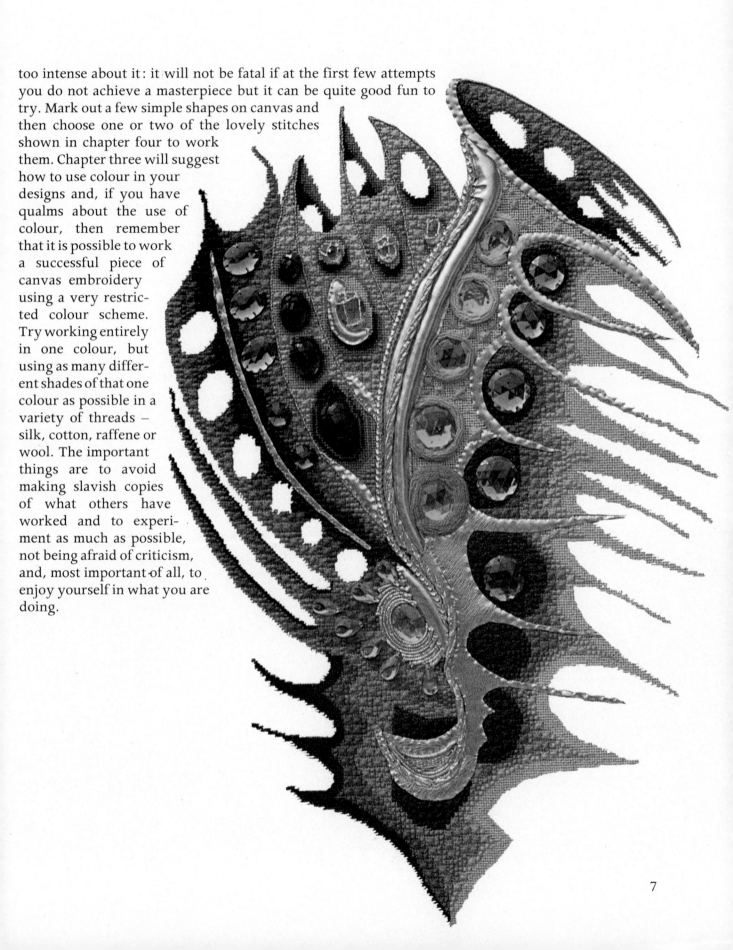

too intense about it: it will not be fatal if at the first few attempts you do not achieve a masterpiece but it can be quite good fun to try. Mark out a few simple shapes on canvas and then choose one or two of the lovely stitches shown in chapter four to work them. Chapter three will suggest how to use colour in your designs and, if you have qualms about the use of colour, then remember that it is possible to work a successful piece of canvas embroidery using a very restricted colour scheme. Try working entirely in one colour, but using as many different shades of that one colour as possible in a variety of threads – silk, cotton, raffene or wool. The important things are to avoid making slavish copies of what others have worked and to experiment as much as possible, not being afraid of criticism, and, most important of all, to enjoy yourself in what you are doing.

1 The history of canvas embroidery

Embroidery is a very ancient craft which existed, along with weaving, in the earliest recorded period of human history in Egypt and Assyria, in China, India and Persia, and was probably first associated with the decoration of garments.

The actual form of the earliest embroideries is difficult to establish exactly, but they were probably pieces of work done with stitchery upon an existing background material, similar to what would today be called crewel work. The background materials were probably even-weave linen or cotton fabric with the embroidery worked in silk, cotton or fine wool.

At some point in the evolution of modern embroidery, a coarser linen fabric was introduced as ground material and this necessitated the use of thicker embroidery thread in order to cover the ground adequately. Woollen thread, which has a greater covering power than silk or cotton, was the natural one to use for this purpose, and it also became customary to work over the whole area of the coarser background fabric.

This method of working over the whole of the background is what finally made canvas work different from all other types of embroidery. Today we do, of course, find experimental pieces of canvas work in which the entire background fabric is not worked over, but this is only a recent development and is a part of the modern tendency to discard traditionally accepted rules and to work in complete freedom.

'Tobias and the Angel' Flemish, mid-sixteenth century. The last three scenes of a very long, narrow panel of seven scenes, depicting the story of Tobias and the Angel. The whole panel is worked in wool, silk and metal threads.

The early European tradition

Europe has a long history of canvas work in England and in France principally, but also in Spain, Italy and Germany. A very fine tradition of the work exists in England, but unfortunately only a few examples of the earliest period still remain. One such example is seen in the heraldic orphrey on the famous Syon Cope, which dates from the late thirteenth century and is now in the Victoria and Albert Museum in London; another example is a corporal case belonging to Wymondham Abbey in Norfolk, England, which is said to date from the early fourteenth century. Further examples, also in the Victoria and Albert Museum, are a purse and two seal bags on a charter of 1319 and the Calthorpe Purse (shown on page 10), dated at about 1540. A number of canvas embroidered book-bindings have also survived and the earliest is in the British Museum in London. It is attached to a famous thirteenth century manuscript, the Felbrigge Psalter, but the binding itself is of the fourteenth century. This is probably the oldest known example of an embroidered binding in existence. It depicts the Annunciation on the front cover and the Crucifixion on the back and is worked in silk of various colours with fine gold thread for the background. Unfortunately, its present condition is very poor, and there are no photographs of it suitable for reproduction. I have prepared a colour drawing of the front cover to show how it probably looked

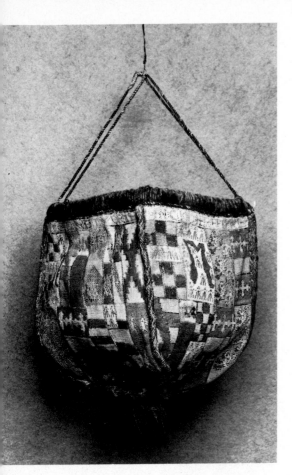

The Calthorpe Purse, mid-sixteenth century. This purse which has four shield-shaped side panels exhibiting the coats of arms of the Calthorpe family, was probably used as an alms-bag or a decorative holder for presents of money or jewellery to be given to friends or to royalty at the New Year. It is worked in tent stitch on very fine linen canvas, having approximately 1,250 stitches to the square inch. △

A panel of canvas work which is to be incorporated into a leather binding for a bible. Tent stitch has been used to work this panel instead of the split stitch on the original binding, and the canvas used here is also much coarser than that of the original, which was a pliable, fairly loosely-woven linen. ▷

when first worked. The photograph on page 11 shows a recent panel of similar size, on coarser canvas, based on this drawing.

Sixteenth-century magnificence

Apart from these few examples, there was apparently no large output of English canvas work before about 1560 and the beginning of the Elizabethan period proper, when there suddenly occurred a great eruption of work which produced many magnificent examples. Some of the smaller pieces were probably done by amateurs, but most of the magnificent large table carpets, hangings and valances of the period (see pages 12 and 13) reveal a standard of workmanship of such perfection that they must have been produced by skilled professionals. They were worked with wool and silk and mainly in tent stitch, the fashionable stitch of the time and which in fact remained a firm favourite right up to the eighteenth century. Cushion and chair-seat covers and carpets to cover cupboard and chest tops, as well as covers for books, became very popular, and many were worked on canvas, which proved a good, strong fabric for the purpose.

Elizabethan embroidery design generally favoured all-over patterns, and most of the canvas work of this period, which was done on linen canvas with a mesh of 16 or 18 threads to the inch, was very fine and achieved a mass of detail leaving very little background space unembellished. It was as if the designers had a horror of undecorated space, and they filled an embroidered panel with intricate representations of natural forms of all kinds, flowers, leaves, fruit and tendrils, animals, birds and groups of elaborately costumed human figures. A special feature of many of these Elizabethan pieces is the extensive use of strap work to divide up a panel and to frame various sections of the design.

Sometimes the motifs for a design were worked individually on canvas and were then applied upon a ground material such as velvet. The famous hangings (see panel on page 12) of Oxburgh Hall in Norfolk, England, some portions of which are kept in the Victoria and Albert Museum in London were worked in this manner by Mary, Queen of Scots, and Elizabeth, Countess of Shrewsbury, in about 1570. A long cushion cover of the same period, also on show at the Victoria and Albert Museum, has similarly worked motifs mounted on a velvet background.

A special type of canvas work which appeared in England in the sixteenth century was Turkey work. Double strands of wool were passed through the canvas and knotted. The wool was then clipped very short on the front of the work to form a close pile rather like that of the Oriental carpets which this kind of embroidery was in fact seeking to imitate. Turkey work was widely used for such things as cushion and bench covers, as well as for the so-called 'foot carpetts' of the period, and the designs employed were usually all-over floral patterns, worked in many colours and with only small areas of background showing.

Designs become simpler

As the seventeenth century progressed, canvas work at first continued very much in the Elizabethan tradition but gradually, however, a change took place. The size of individual pieces of work tended to decrease and the designs became simpler and less

extravagant than they had been in the previous century. Small panels were now produced with simple, open designs, showing scenes based on Bible stories or classical mythology in which human figures, animals, trees and buildings were depicted against a background of fields and sky. Little regard was shown for proportion or perspective and animal or bird shapes were often used quite indiscriminately merely to fill an empty space in the design. Certain of these designs, such as that showing Adam and Eve in the Garden of Eden or Abraham talking to the Angels, (shown on page 17), became so popular that they were repeated on panels over and over again.

Elizabethan Bed Valances, late sixteenth century. The Elizabethan bed chamber was an important room in which much entertaining of guests took place, and among the wealthy it was lavishly furnished with elaborately-worked embroideries such as these valances. They are worked in tent stitch with a few simulated pearls worked in raised stitch. ▷

The Oxburgh Hangings. A panel from the Oxburgh hangings, embroidered in about 1570 by Elizabeth, Countess of Shrewsbury, and Mary, Queen of Scots, and their ladies. The motifs are worked in tent, cross and long-legged cross stitches on linen canvas in silk and silver-gilt thread and are applied to a green velvet background which has a design in cord couched all over it. ◁

A detail of a cushion showing the arms of Norwich. This is a very fine example of Turkey work carried out on a coarse linen canvas. ▷

(Illustrations on pages 14 and 15)
Summer. This is a large hanging produced in France in 1683–84. It is worked on canvas in wool and silk, with a background of metal thread. It is probably one of a set representing the Seasons, and the design is without doubt taken from a Gobelin tapestry.

A mid-nineteenth century Victorian cushion with an attractive design, showing two cherubs sitting on a cloud. Originally it had a silk background, which has now completely rotted and worn away. It has been made up with a knotted cord all round.

A typical late Victorian cushion, showing a couple of cabbage roses and an enormous arum lily. It is worked in wool and silk with a beaded background of coarse silver beads.

This pulpit fall is an attractive, well-balanced design, using conventionalized floral motifs.

13

Embroidery in the home

During the seventeenth century, English embroiderers were still working bookbindings and cushion and chair-seat covers but other things, such as workboxes and caskets of various kinds, as well as mirror surrounds, purses and pincushions, became popular objects for decorating with embroidery. Tent stitch on canvas was still being used and the work, which was carried out either in silk or in silk and wool upon a fine, strong canvas, produced such an exceedingly durable finish that very many specimens have survived to this day to delight us.

Early samplers

Many beautifully worked samplers appeared at this time also and these bear a number of small, detached motifs, which are either purely geometric patterns or conventional floral shapes, worked upon a linen background like a very fine canvas. The embroidery is worked in tent stitch and cross stitch, with the occasional use of rococo stitch and sometimes, in later examples, of florentine stitch. The early samplers were probably made by the embroiderers as permanent records of stitches and of certain motifs they might wish to repeat but later samplers, which were often dated and bore the name of the worker, seem to have been exercises done by beginners.

Oriental influences

The last twenty years of the seventeenth century brought a great change in embroidery design in England with the introduction of oriental styles which had been fashionable in Holland for some

16

Part of a long cushion cover, mid-seventeenth century, showing Abraham and the Angels. This cushion is worked in tent stitch, with the hair of the angels in bullion stitch. ▷

This book cover, which shows on the front a picture of Abraham about to sacrifice Isaac, was worked in the year 1613 by Elizabeth Illingworthe. On the back cover is a scene of Jonah and the Whale. It is worked in silk on linen canvas in tent stitch with some bullion stitch and a few french knots. ◁

A purse of the late sixteenth or early seventeenth century. This strange-looking little purse is worked in the form of a bunch of grapes. It is worked on canvas with coloured silks and metal thread. Such fancy shapes as this were not uncommon for purses at this time. ◁

A canvas work purse with pincushion attachment. This attractive little bag from the early seventeenth century, fastened with plaited draw-strings and a cord for hanging, is finished with tassels. It is worked with silk in tent stitch on a background of plaited stitch in silver thread. The small pincushion has a foliated diamond enclosing a rose with four hearts-ease flowers, one at each corner. ▷

years previously. Such styles in design now became very popular both as a result of the contact with the Dutch royal house and also through the increasing trade with the East. The floral designs of this period show a noticeable difference from earlier work in the size of the flowers and leaves, which became much bigger and bolder. They were also beautifully shaded, being worked in tent stitch with silk to render the highlights. Work of this kind was in general .beautifully designed and executed, the canvas usually being of a somewhat coarser mesh than formerly to suit the bolder designs. As well as these largely floral designs, canvas embroidery in the late seventeenth century also included examples of that strange mixture of oriental and western styles called Chino-Dutch. This was a design built up by using many interlocking abstract shapes, worked in a variety of colours mainly in gros point, (tent stitch worked over two threads of the canvas), or cross stitch. Even in the early eighteenth century, the oriental influence was still apparent in some of the designs produced but the best examples of English canvas work were still based, as in earlier times, on all-over floral designs in tent stitch. The same well-known flowers were used, tulips, roses, honeysuckle and carnations, but there was now a tendency towards greater naturalism in the designs.

Pieces of canvas embroidery of similar design and comparable in workmanship were also being produced in France at this time, where a strong and persistent tradition of such work was established.

Florentine or Bargello work

In the early eighteenth century a zig-zag stitch known as florentine or flame stitch – sometimes called hungarian point or bargello work became extremely popular and was used for working large bed hangings, valances and furniture coverings. The actual origin of this stitch is not known, but it is thought to have been introduced from Italy as early as the sixteenth century. Its popularity might well have been associated with the fact that florentine stitch is very quick to work, and is also an economical method of embroidering large hangings and furniture coverings. This type of canvas embroidery was also taken across the Atlantic to the colonies of the New World, where it became similarly very popular and many examples of American florentine work still exist. These were produced about the middle of the eighteenth century, and some good examples can be seen in the Metropolitan Museum of Art in New York. Similar designs were being produced at the same time in many European countries.

Shepherds and Shepherdesses

During the second half of the eighteenth century several changes took place in canvas embroidery both in design and in the manner of working. Scenes from biblical and classical stories, which had been popular at the beginning of the century, gradually gave way to pastoral scenes with gaily dressed shepherds and shepherdesses sitting around under shady trees and minding their woolly lambs.

There was also a gradual change in the all-over type of floral design for canvas work, which had been popular since Tudor days. Gradually the floral motifs ceased to be used to form a close all-

18

Chinoiserie panel. Part of a large panel, late seventeenth century, worked entirely in tent stitch and mainly in wool. ◁

A detail of a sampler of stitches and stitch patterns of the early seventeenth century which is worked in coloured silks and metal thread in a variety of stitches including tent and rococo. The length of this panel is 2 feet 6 inches and it is 11½ inches wide. The two holes in this sampler – recently very skilfully repaired – were probably occasioned by the removal of the motifs for applying on another background. ▽

A pastoral scene entitled 'The Reclining Shepherd' worked by Hannah Goddard in New England in the mid-eighteenth century. This panel shows a very strong European influence, although it is rather more naïve in treatment than would have been similar European pieces of the same time.

over pattern and were instead spread around in the form of sprays or powderings of natural flowers upon the background area.

Canvas work, which had been so extensively used for furniture coverings in the past now began to give way to the new fashion of using patterned textiles, brocades, plain silks and damasks for furnishings. Sometimes however, small panels or motifs were worked on canvas and then cut out and applied to a woven fabric which was intended for covering a chair-seat or cushion. This was either done in the same way as was customary when small pieces of canvas work were mounted upon a different ground material in Tudor times, or sometimes an area of canvas was first tacked on to the ground material and tent stitch was then worked through both the canvas and the ground material. The threads of the canvas were afterwards withdrawn, when the embroidery had been completed.

During the latter part of the eighteenth century, there was a general decline in the quality of embroidery in England and although needlework was still displayed on small articles such as pole-screens, hand-screens and candle-screens, as well as on card tables and occasionally on wall panels, there was a definite falling-off in its use. This is further emphasized by the fact that canvas work being produced in France in the same period shows a marked superiority over any contemporary English work, both in design and in technique.

Berlin wool work

There was no improvement in standards of taste and design in

English canvas embroidery of the nineteenth century, but a change in style occurred, which emanated from Germany and was to affect canvas work design throughout much of Europe, as well as in America, for many years to come. In 1804, a print-seller in Berlin issued the first coloured needlework design on squared paper. This enabled anyone to work a piece of embroidery by mechanically copying the design, square by square, on to open-meshed canvas, and it very soon became extremely popular. Another Berlin print- and bookseller named Wittich was induced by his wife to extend his business by printing many copies of such patterns; numerous other print publishers joined in what soon became a very remunerative business, and between 1810 and 1840 no less than 14,000 different copper-plate designs of this kind were produced. Germany was of course the first country to produce considerable amounts of needlework based on the new designs, but Russia, England, France, America, Sweden, Denmark and Holland soon followed, the first two being, after Germany, by far the largest exponents of the new style.

The new designs were at first worked chiefly in silk. Later, beads were introduced and finally a soft wool yarn became the principal material in which the new embroidery was carried out. The wool, which was produced in Gotha, was dyed with the new aniline dyes in Berlin, and this gave a name to the style of embroidery, which has ever since been called Berlin wool work.

Although France imported numbers of the Berlin patterns, many French ladies still preferred to work according to their old-established method from designs previously traced on to canvas

A canvas work chair seat of the early nineteenth century, showing the type of embroidery that was worked from a printed chart by counting the stitches.

This panel, which is entitled 'Domestic Happiness', was worked in the middle of the nineteenth century from one of the thousands of printed colour charts which were very popular from 1840 onwards. It is worked on double-thread canvas, but the double threads have been displaced to enable the cat and her kittens and the faces and hands of the human figures to be worked more finely over the single threads.

21

and their work, which had already attained a position of superiority in Europe during the latter part of the eighteenth century, continued to hold that position during the nineteenth century.

In England, merchants and industrialists had begun to amass great fortunes and, wishing to emulate the landed gentry, encouraged their wives to produce embroidery with which to decorate their homes. Their experience of life, however, had not fitted the ladies to choose what was best in design. They were enthusiastic about the Berlin wool patterns and the general quality of all embroidery design in England was consequently lowered even further.

By the middle of the nineteenth century the flood gates were open, and there was such an outpouring of canvas work as had not been seen since the seventeenth century. The quantity of printed charts for working on canvas in cross stitch or gros point – two much-favoured stitches of the period – was now so vast that it sounded the death-knell to all good design and technique.

It now became the fashion of the day to work different furnishings for each piece of furniture rather than to work whole sets of matching furnishings, as had formerly been the custom. A single chair, cushion, stool, hassock or screen would be covered with a design consisting of a wreath or bunch of large cabbage roses, arum lilies and other flowers and worked in the soft, fluffy, crudely-coloured German wools. Small articles, such as pincushions, slippers for both men and women, small hand screens, boxes, bags and practically every other thing it was possible to cover with canvas work, were covered in Berlin woolwork.

In America, very little canvas work had been done up to the nineteenth century. The needlework done by the women settlers was mainly in the form of patchwork and appliqué and was directed by the necessity of conserving their materials and by economy. Canvas work was considered a luxury needlecraft. A small amount of canvas work was brought into America from Europe during the eighteenth century, but it was not until the nineteenth century that canvas work began to be done in any quantity. The large influx of immigrants from Europe, and particularly from Germany, quite naturally brought with it the popular Berlin woolwork of the time, and traces of this design style can still be seen in the canvas embroidery being produced in America at the present day.

A wind of change

From about 1860 to the end of the century a British craftsman-designer named William Morris and his associates contributed to a movement which endeavoured to bring about a revival of good decorative art in Britain. The ideas of this group had a considerable effect upon the embroidery of the late nineteenth century and led to an upsurge of interest in what was then called art needlework. Various societies were founded in the 1870s and 1880s to promote this new needlework, and, as a result, there was a revival of interest with some contemporary designs being used, but largely with designs adapted from seventeenth century work, using muted colour schemes suggested by the faded appearance of the 200-year-old pieces.

But in spite of the efforts of William Morris and his followers,

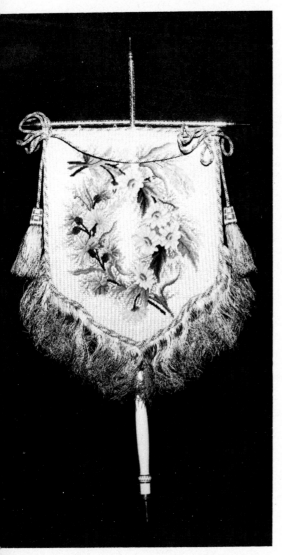

One of a pair of delightful little hand-screens made in France during the first half of the nineteenth century. They were worked on a fine canvas of 28 threads to the inch, and the design was carried out in tent stitch on a cream silk background of long cross stitches worked horizontally. Such hand-screens were used to protect the complexions of ladies from the intense heat of open fires.

Church kneeler, a modern development of a traditional type of design.

European and American embroidery design remained rather uninspired throughout the first quarter of the twentieth century. Reproductions of past styles in canvas work continued to be faithfully made by professionals, using the original pieces as their models, but the amateur embroiderer still relied mainly upon the commercially produced designs. A great deal of the work done by amateurs still showed the influences of the worst of nineteenth century design.

Improved design and workmanship

After the Second World War, a new and much improved type of canvas work began to emerge. Interest in embroidery of all kinds had been encouraged by many educational organizations in both Britain and America to raise the standard of design and workmanship in the craft, as well as to encourage its general development. As a result, people began to seek new and exciting ways of doing canvas embroidery. There has been a tendency, as in other types of embroidery, to produce purely decorative pieces of work, and framed pictures embroidered on canvas have replaced many of the more utilitarian pieces of former days. Good traditional canvas work continues to be done for the Church, using both traditional and contemporary designs (see Pulpit fall, page 15). In secular work, designs have moved away from the traditional floral patterns of the past towards a more abstract style; and more emphasis is placed on obtaining pleasing textural effects by using a great variety of stitches. Colouring has become brighter once again and new and unusual threads are used, together with materials such as metallic cords, gold and silver leather, jewels, various types of string and velvet ribbons.

23

2 Designing canvas embroidery

There are two distinct types of design for canvas embroidery, the geometric type of all-over count stitch pattern, which is very suitable for the working of covers for stool-tops, chair seats and cushions, and the completely free type of design, whether pictorial or abstract, which is used mostly for wall panels and hangings.

No elaborate design is required for the working of a count stitch pattern, but a simple chart is often used as a guide to the worker. The only skill that is needed is the ability to count the threads accurately, but it does demand infinite patience and concentration if mistakes are to be avoided.

Good designs already traced upon canvas are available for the embroiderer who desires to do something freer and more creative than the working of count stitch patterns, but I should like to stress that I am not referring to the coloured or tramméd canvases available in many needlework shops which are merely poor imitations of the embroideries of former days or attempts to reproduce in embroidery certain well-known paintings. What I have in mind are those prepared canvases which are clearly the work of professional designers and based on good modern designs. We have an enormous selection of modern materials to choose from, including the lovely lurex threads and other new man-made fibres, so that it should prove easy for modern embroiderers to experiment with new ideas and to work designs that suit the new age and the new materials.

Eventually those embroiderers who want to be truly creative and to produce a completely original piece of canvas embroidery should be persuaded to make a design for themselves. I meet many who, when faced with the suggestion of producing their own designs, shake their heads and murmur to themselves, 'That is not for me'. To them I always say that the problem is by no means so insurmountable as they at first imagine. Design is simply the art of placing lines and shapes in an orderly manner within a certain background area and of balancing one shape against another, using lines where necessary to link up the separate parts of the whole. In building up a design in this way the would-be designer needs to watch carefully that the areas of background left between shapes in the design should themselves be well-balanced and have an attractive appearance. It helps for instance if shapes cut out of paper are being used to create a design, to place these shapes upon a background of a different colour. Alternatively, if a design is being drawn up on paper, paint in the background with a thin wash of colour. In this way it is not difficult to make sure that the background areas form a pleasant, well-balanced pattern and that the balance between design shapes and background shapes is correct: beginners often tend to leave background areas too large in comparison with the areas of pattern and thus spoil the balance of the whole design.

1a. A design abstracted from the photograph of the dried flower head. Suitable stitches to use in working the design might be rice stitch, smyrna, chequer and oblong cross stitch with tent stitch, hungarian or small diagonal stitch for the background. Outline everything in tent stitch first. ▷

1. Dried flower head. A small section of this photograph could be developed into a design for canvas work. ▷

24

Sources of designs
Natural Objects

Anyone with a good sense of design can readily find an idea simply by observing everyday objects as they present themselves. Nature, for instance, has always provided the chief source of ideas for design and the pleasing shapes and lines of plants and flowers can yield an idea for a canvas work design. A good way for the beginner to proceed when seeking an idea from nature is to photograph suitable natural forms. When these pictures are enlarged, some especially interesting detail will often emerge, which will produce an inspiration for a design. This should then be drawn up, but here it is necessary to forget the exact nature and appearance of the original object and to concentrate on the chosen

2a. A possible design developed from the denuded flower head.

2. Here the flower head is finally denuded of all its petals. It is still beautiful, and its centre could provide the inspiration for a canvas work design. ▽

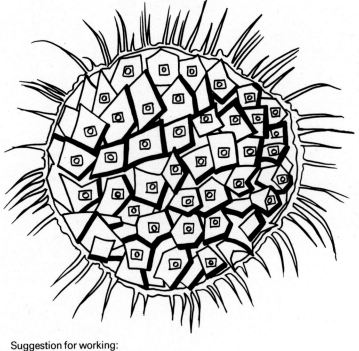

Suggested stitches
- ∿ small diagonal
- ⫼ hungarian
- ✕ rice
- ▦ chequer
- ✳ smyrna
- ✕ oblong cross

Suggestion for working:
thick lines: smyrna stitch
thin lines: tent stitch
◙ eyelets
background of centre: mosaic stitch
spiky surround: tent stitch

3. Shells and skeleton shells can provide endless ideas for design. This enlarged photograph shows clearly the pure, sculptural lines.▽

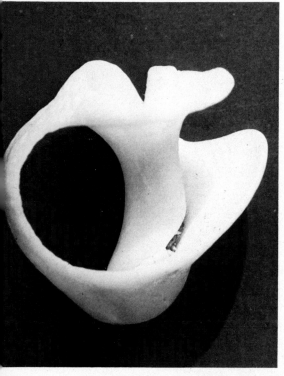

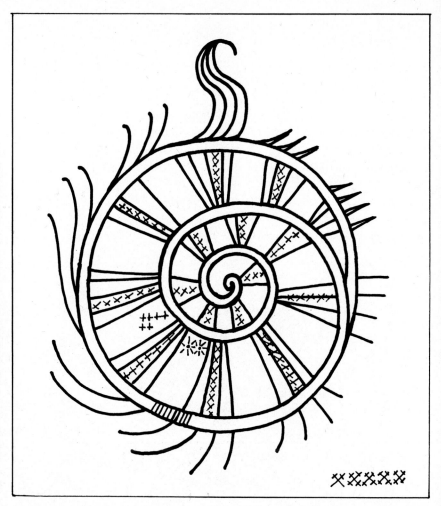

4. 'Skeleton shell'. This design was adapted from a picture of a skeleton shell and is worked in smyrna, cross stitch and french knots on a background of hungarian stitch, with beads and gold leather applied. ▽

section, altering and developing it until it will form the basis of a design (Illustrations 1–6).

A note-book is an essential piece of equipment for the would-be designer, so that sketches can be made at any time of objects which appeal as possible sources of a design. The sketches should be made as accurate as possible for, although they will not be used to produce a design which is a faithful copy of the original object, they do provide material from which one section can be isolated and developed in the same way as with photographs. It is helpful to make small sketches of the chosen object from many different angles until one suitable for a specific purpose is discovered. A tracing of this final sketch should then be made, showing only the principal lines of the original, which can then be developed in one's own way as an embroidery design. Sometimes, if a first tracing appears to be too complicated to give a good design, a second tracing can be made from it with the object of reducing the mass of lines even further, and thus simplifying the idea. One should try to find a good, simple foundation upon which a design suitable for working on canvas can be built up.

Not only will nature prove a useful store-house for ideas for the embroidery designer, but inspiration can also be drawn from the mass of man-made objects which surround us: buildings, machinery, furniture, doors and windows, motorcars and aeroplanes can provide inspiration for designs, whether geometric or free.

5. Fern frond. The coiled-up leaf of a fern offers us inspiration for designs based on the circle. ◁

5a. A design developed from the picture of the fern fond. As a suggestion for working, everything could be outlined in tent stitch; cross stitch or any other solid-looking stitch used for the 'spokes'; Algerian and straight cross stitch for the spaces in between. The rim could be padded with string and satin stitch worked over it. The background could be worked in rice or cashmere stitch. ◁◁

Paper shapes

For anyone who has difficulty in drawing designs upon paper, a good way of designing is that of the old, well-tried method of cutting or tearing shapes out of paper and using these to build up a suitable design (as shown in illustration 9). The shapes can be placed either on a background sheet of paper or on the actual canvas itself and moved around within the area chosen for the design until a satisfactory arrangement is found. Thin tissue paper is good for this purpose, as the shapes can be overlapped, one showing through another, thus adding variety by suggesting gradations of tone, which may even help towards the eventual choice of a colour scheme. To achieve greater originality in a design try not to place the shapes carefully in position at the start, but drop them at random on to the chosen background area and only then make adjustments to achieve a proper balance. This avoids any predisposition one might have to arrange the design always in a similar, perhaps rather restricted way. When the shapes are arranged satisfactorily, trace them off if they have been placed on a background of paper. If the shapes have been arranged upon the canvas itself, pin them into position and paint round the outlines with a brush and black water colour paint or a felt-tipped pen. There is a danger, however, if a felt-tipped pen is used, that the colour may rub off on to light-coloured threads.

Not only can shapes cut out of paper be arranged to form a design, but suggestions for designs – particularly for the geometric type of pattern – can also be obtained from sheets of paper by folding them and cutting out shapes with scissors, working always from the folded edge inwards. When unfolded the sheets of paper will often reveal interesting patterns, which may be used for canvas work (illustrations 7–11).

6. This photograph shows the detail of the inner lining of the eggshell, which, with the curves and shadows of the outer shape, offers almost a ready-made design. △

7. Cut-paper design formed by folding a square of greaseproof paper in half vertically, horizontally and diagonally and cutting out shapes from the folded edges inwards. △

8. Cut-paper design formed by cutting two folded squares. The top square was cut from the folded edge of the paper and the other from the unfolded edge. △

9. Squares of decreasing size, cut out of newspaper, have been placed one on top of another, alternate shapes being turned to form diamonds. The light and dark areas of the newsprint can suggest a variety of texture. ◁

10a. A design taken from a section on the lower right-hand side of the re-assembled advertisement, illustration 10. The abstracted shape was drawn up on tracing paper, which was then folded in two vertically and the lines traced through. The paper was then opened out, folded in two horizontally and the lines traced through again. A simple design was thus evolved. Bold shapes like these are ideal for canvas work, where all extra details needed are achieved by the choice of attractive stitches. ▷

11. Revolving triangles. A small panel based on a cut-paper design. ◁

10. An advertisement in bold type has been cut into strips and re-assembled and has made a pattern which could be worked in a limited colour scheme. The whole design could be outlined with a wide band of stitchery, which would help to bind it together, or alternatively a 'finder' might be used on it to isolate a small section, which could then be enlarged. ▽

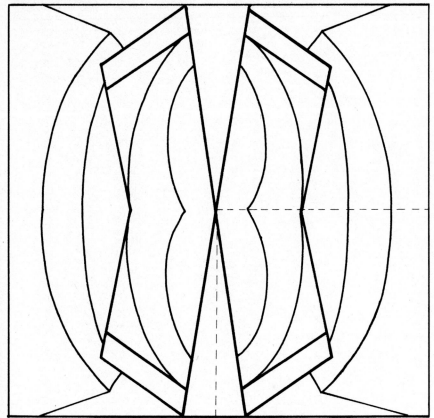

29

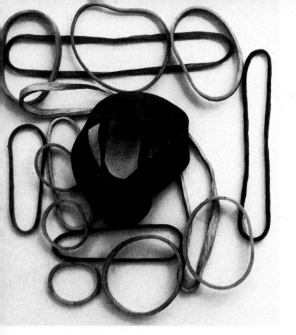

Inspiration from household articles

Designs can also be discovered by grouping and arranging such things as match-boxes, paper clips, wood shavings and sections of objects such as cartons, polythene bottles and pieces of corrugated paper. Drawings and photographs of suitable arrangements of things of this kind can be very helpful in finding the best design for a specific purpose (illustrations 12–16).

A further useful source of designs for embroidery is to be found by cutting cross-sections of fruit or vegetables or of the seed heads of flowers. If these sections are examined carefully under a magnifying glass, they will often reveal interesting ideas for designs. Sometimes it is a good idea to place such cross-sections of fruits or seed heads between pieces of glass to make slides which can be projected upon a screen, where they will give a useful black and white image (illustration 14). A photograph of such a projected image may be used to provide the final basis for a design.

Reflections and shadows of objects upon a wall, the ceiling or floor can be a lively and quite exciting source of designs, as can also the tracery of a tree against the sky or its shadow on a wall.

Ideas for designs can be obtained from advertisements or pictures in magazines by using a 'finder'. This is a piece of card with a circular or rectangular aperture cut out of it. Place the finder upon a chosen picture so that it isolates a small section, which can then be drawn up, enlarged and developed to give a design (illustrations 15 and 15a). Photographs from science magazines prove a useful source of inspiration (illustrations 20–23, pages

12. Rubber bands. Rubber bands of all sizes such as the large, wide band in the centre, can be helpful in suggesting a geometric type of design.

13. The reflection of a wine glass standing in the sunshine.

38–39).

The important thing about looking for a design is to be constantly alert to the possibilities offered by the vast number of objects which surround us, but it is also important to realize that the most satisfactory modern designs will not result from a purely naturalistic representation of the original object chosen, but from the development of certain shapes and lines which are abstracted from it.

'Found objects' as part of a design

Not only can 'found objects' of various kinds provide ideas from which canvas work designs may be developed, but such things can also sometimes be employed themselves as actual parts of a design, by attaching them to the surface of the canvas and building the remainder of the design around them with suitable stitchery (see pages 40 and 41). Interesting pieces of stone or shells collected from the beach are excellent for this purpose, and beads and jewels, singly or in groups, can also be used to form a centre of interest from which to develop an exciting design on canvas.

Cutting holes in the canvas

Sometimes a design has been developed around a centre of interest formed by cutting holes in the surface of the canvas to allow such things as coloured glass and attractive pieces of metal to be seen through them (see page 33, below). When this was first suggested, it was regarded as a rather daring innovation, but today it is quite

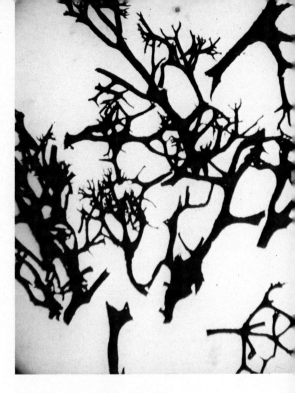

14. A photograph of the projected image of a slide made from flower stalks.

74

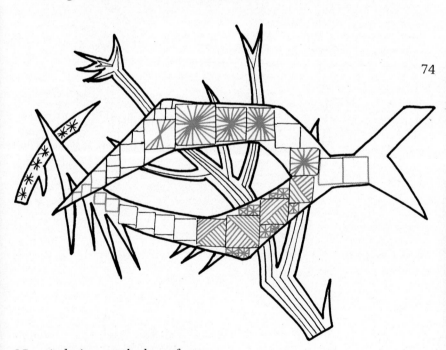

15a. A design worked out from the idea obtained by using the 'finder'. As indicated on the design, any large square stitch could be used to appropriate size. Refer to the chapter on stitchery to choose the stitches.

15. A 'finder' being used to select a section of the photograph which was projected on the screen.

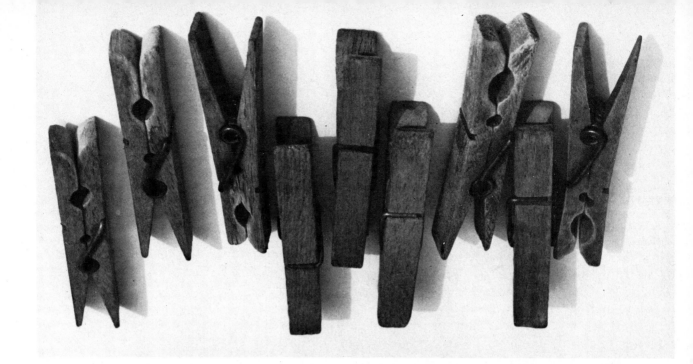

16. Clothes pins. A row of pins after the laundry has been taken in. △

16a. A sketch made from the row of pins is suitable as a design for a collar. ▷

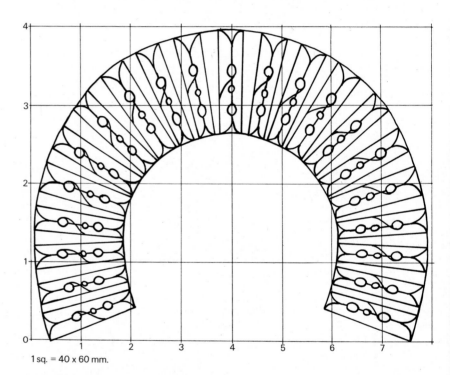

1 sq. = 40 x 60 mm.

(opposite page):
A small piece of the pin design for a collar worked on canvas, see also illustrations 16 and 16a.

A detail of a panel based on a cut-paper design. Interesting features are the holes which have been cut out and coloured glass put behind; the use of interesting threads and materials such as gold, leather and creosoted string and the effect of the double knot stitch.

32

acceptable and, for those who enjoy experimenting, it may well provide an exciting experience.

Designs based on stitchery

It is possible to create interesting designs by simply using the stitchery itself as an inspiration: good geometric patterns especially can be built up by the simple process of working groups of stitches and repeating them at regular intervals over the canvas.

Enlarging a design

Sometimes it becomes necessary to enlarge a design in order to make it suitable for working upon canvas. This is not a difficult task, if the drawing is enclosed within a square or rectangle, which

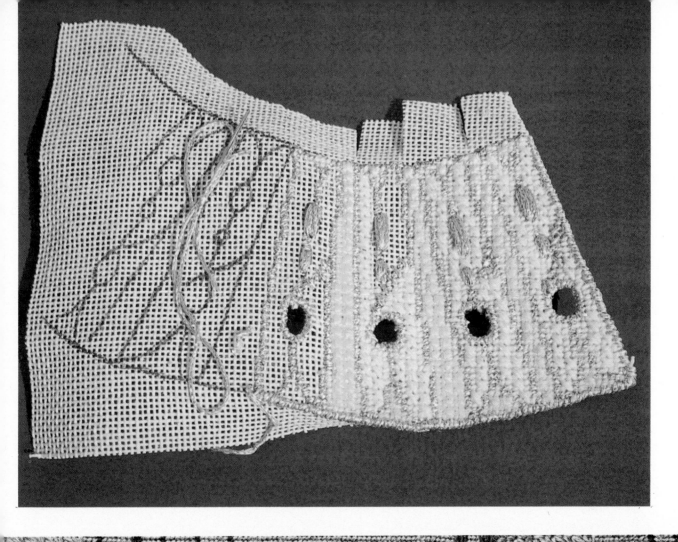

is then divided up into a grid of squares (illustration 18). A tracing of the original design can be used in order not to spoil the original design by drawing lines across it (illustration 17). The grid of squares should be numbered from the bottom left-hand corner both vertically and horizontally. A rectangle of the size required for the piece of work should be drawn up on a larger sheet of paper and divided into a grid in a similar way. These larger squares should also be numbered from the bottom left-hand corner both vertically and horizontally. If it is desired to double the size of the design, this is easily done if the small drawing is covered with a grid of half-inch squares and the larger paper has a grid of one-inch squares; if the design is to be three times larger than the original, then, with the smaller drawing having a grid of half-inch squares, the large rectangle should be divided into one-and-a-half inch squares, and so on. The enlarged drawing of the design is made by carefully matching the position of the lines on the enlarged grid with those of the original design on the smaller grid.

If the enlarged design has to fit a size which cannot readily be expressed as a multiple of the measurements of the small design, this can be overcome without too much trouble. If, for instance, a drawing which is $6\frac{1}{4}$ inches long has to be extended to 15 inches long, the smaller rectangle can be drawn, and the side AB extended to E, so that AE is 15 inches in length (illustration 18). A perpendicular is erected at point E and the diagonal of the original rectangle AC should be extended until it cuts the perpendicular at point F. By extending the side AD of the smaller rectangle until it is equal in length with EF, the larger rectangle AEFG can now be

17. The original drawing for the 'Skeleton shell' design, shown in illustration 4, showing the method of enlarging.

34

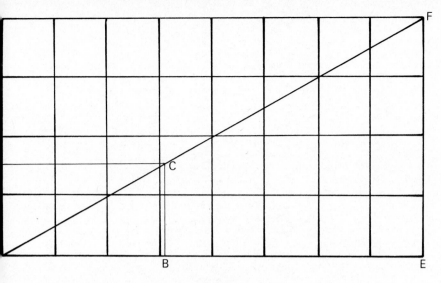

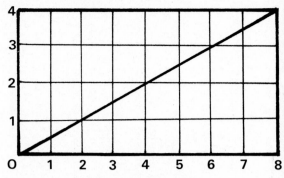

18. *The method of enlarging a drawing to a certain fixed length or width.* △

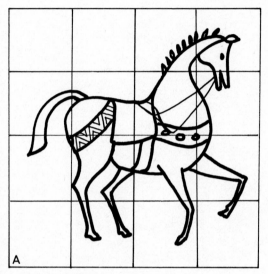

19. *A method of enlarging which also adds some distortion to the original design. (A) shows vertical distortion (B) shows horizontal distortion.*

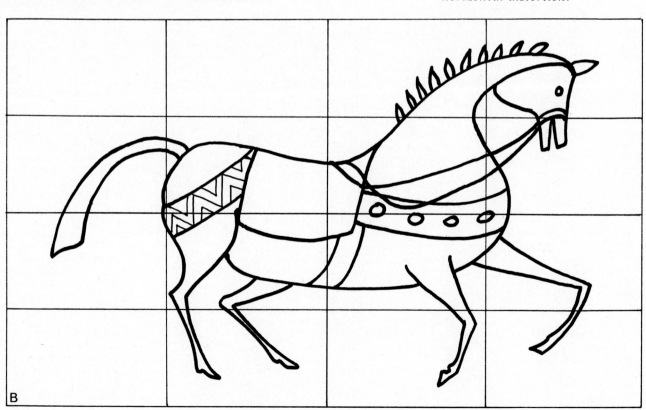

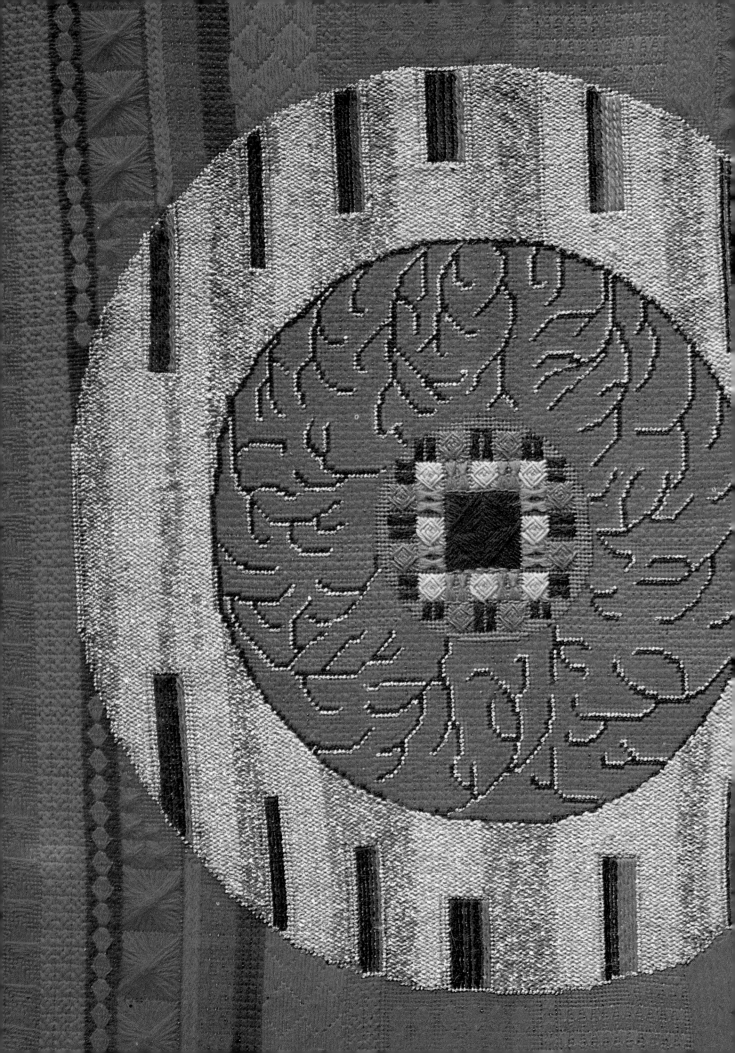

'Summer reflection'. A worked panel based on the reflection from a wine glass, see also illustration 13. ▽

'Circles and Squares'. A worked panel based on an idea from the photograph in the science magazine, illustration 21. ◁

37

20. A photograph, showing
interesting pattern formation,
from a science magazine. ▷

21. Another photograph taken
from a science magazine. ▽

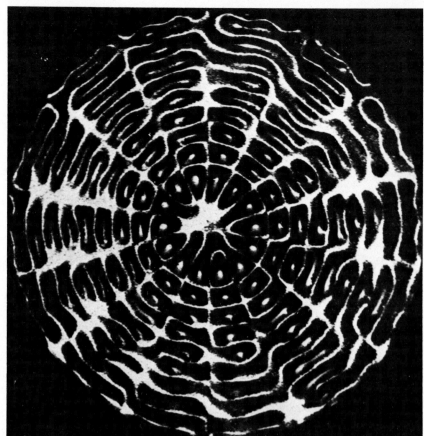

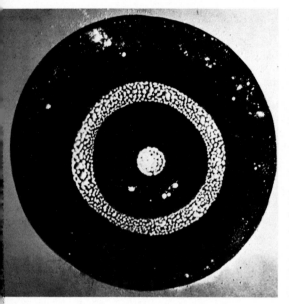

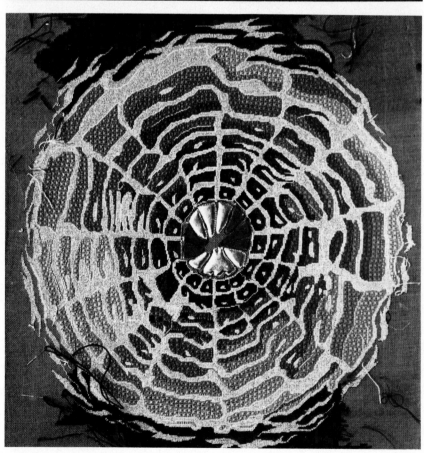

22. A partly worked panel based
on the photograph, illustration
20. △

38

completed. The two rectangles are best divided into a suitable grid by folding them into halves or quarters or perhaps into eighths.

This method of enlarging or reducing an original design also provides the possibility of adding a form of distortion to a design by extending its dimensions more in one direction than in the other, either vertically or horizontally (illustration 19). If, for example, a design such as that shown in illustration 19a were to be extended horizontally and at the same time to be slightly enlarged vertically, the new shape (19b) could be divided into a grid similar to (19a) by quartering the dimensions of the sides and the design could then be copied as in a simple enlarging exercise, but the shapes involved would be elongated in a horizontal direction. Exactly the same sort of distortion can be achieved by extending the dimensions of the original in a vertical direction.

Producing a design for a special purpose

Special problems arise when canvas work designs are being prepared for various household objects or dress accessories. A design will be affected not only by the particular shape of the object to be covered, but also by the use to which it will be put, as well as by its setting in a room and the way in which it will be viewed when in position. Cushions, stool-tops and rugs require a design which can be viewed equally well from all angles; mirror surrounds are best constructed on a balanced or symmetrical design, which will form a good, flowing, decorative border suited to the shape and table lamp bases of the type depicted on page 127, which are made

23. 'Abstract'. This canvas work panel, which was based on a photograph in a science magazine, gives a three-dimensional effect.

A detail of an unfinished panel, based on groups of stones found on a beach. These were stitched on to the canvas, and the design developed around them with string and woollen yarns. ◁

'Currency Souvenir'. Certain copper coins of the old currency were attached to the canvas and incorporated in a design adapted from a motif on the back of a five-pound note. The coins were attached to the canvas by drilling two small holes near opposite edges of each coin to enable them to be stitched to the background. △

41

by applying a rectangle of canvas embroidery around a cylindrical tube, demand a design that takes full account of the fact that only a small section of the work can be viewed at any one time and from any one angle.

For this last kind of project, designs incorporating vertical lines or bands of horizontally worked stitchery are very effective, as are geometric patterns, as long as the chosen shape fits comfortably into that area of the surface which is visible from the front of the lamp base. Some of the most effective lamp base designs have been achieved merely by starting with a single row of stitches worked vertically, horizontally or diagonally right across the canvas, by varying the stitches and colour over a certain area and then repeating this until the whole shape is covered.

Templates and patterns

In order to prepare a design for working a canvas covering for an existing chair seat or stool top, it is necessary to take a template or pattern (illustrations 24–27). The template for a stool top can be made by placing the stool upside-down in the centre of a large sheet of paper and drawing on the paper all round it by holding a pencil close against the sides of the stool top. This will provide what is called the 'sight-line' which gives the main area within which the design will have to be contained. If the sheet of paper is then folded up around the sides of the stool and a line is drawn on the inner surface of the paper with a pencil laid flat upon the underside of the stool top, the depth of the upholstered top can be marked in. The same process can be employed for taking templates of chair seat squabs, but for a fully upholstered chair place the sheet of

24. Template of a chair seat.

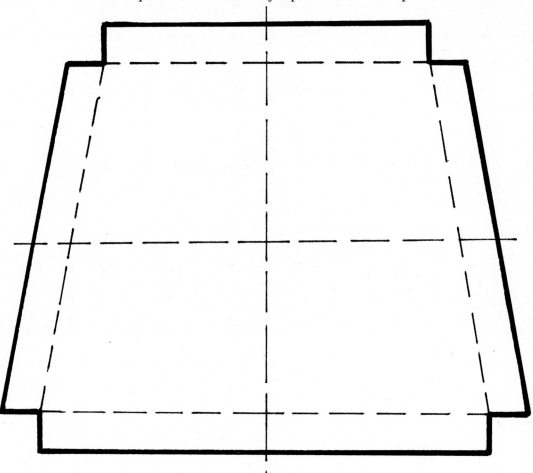

25. Taking a template. A chair squab has been placed face downwards on a sheet of paper, and the pencil is pressed against it, marking in the sight line on the paper. The area thus marked will contain the design to be worked.

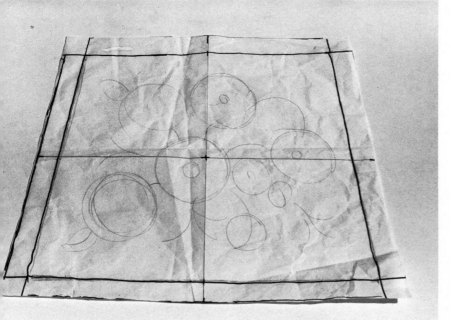

26. The finished template, showing the sight line and the centre lines marked in, and with a suggestion of how the design will be roughed out.

27. A chair seat worked in florentine stitch, showing how the template was marked on the straight of the canvas.

paper over the seat and mark round the edge of the seat with a pencil. Fold the sheet of paper down over the sides and mark the bottom edge of the upholstery in on the paper. Fold the extra paper in at the corners and mark the line where each corner comes on the front, back and at the sides of the seat. Spread the template out and check it to see if the two halves are symmetrical. This is done by folding the template in half from back to front of the seat. If it appears to be asymmetrical, the difference in the outline should be split between the two halves, as the irregularity is probably the result of unevenness in the upholstery, assuming that the actual framework of the chair is quite symmetrical. The template for the chair seat is completed by cutting it out along the outer lines marked on the paper, and it should look something like the paper template shown in illustration 26.

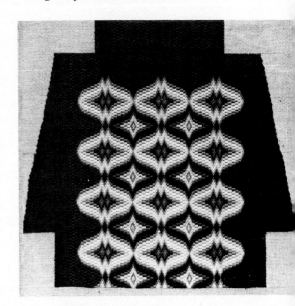

5 Colour and texture

When we first look at a piece of canvas embroidery, our attention is generally held by the colours used in working the design. Some people are immediately attracted by what they regard as the beauty of the colour scheme, while others may find it repellent. Some particularly colour-sensitive people react violently to the slightest colour disharmony, while others accept this readily, welcoming it even as a refreshing innovation, a pleasant departure from the traditional type of colouring associated with such work.

Most of us react in some way to certain colours and tend to associate them with particular human feelings or sensations. Yellow, red and orange are the colours we normally associate with sunshine and warmth: they are glowing colours, which appeal greatly to certain people, who find them gay and cheerful, but they may not be liked in the same way by others who have an antipathy to sunshine and heat. Such people prefer the cooler colours: they are attracted to blue and green, the colours of trees in leaf, grass, water and shade, which others of us may consider cold and depressing.

Everyone is aware of the way in which combinations of different

Tree Bark. By studying the beautiful natural colouring of things such as this tree trunk it is possible to develop a real appreciation of colour, which is most helpful in producing satisfactory colour schemes for embroidery.

A cut-paper explosion. Small pieces of coloured tissue paper of related shapes, arranged at random on a background of contrasting colour, may be just sufficient to stir the imagination and produce an exciting result.

'Colour spiral'. Strong colour contrasts have been used here to give a three-dimensional effect.

45

*'Grey and silver panel'. This
exceedingly striking panel is
worked in silver metallized
thread and six well-graded
shades of grey wool. When
looked at closely, the outer
frame seems to come forward
and the centre square to float in
space. If one continues to look
hard at the panel, the centre
square and the outer frame will
appear to recede and the inner
frame, in its turn, will seem to
float. The stitches used to work
this panel are rhodes, satin and
tent. The size is 28 inches
(70 cm.) square.*

colours can be used to create atmosphere: strong, bold contrasts of
colour can have a very striking and dramatic effect which some
people find exciting, whereas groups of colours, which do not
exhibit the same depth of contrast, can produce a soothing and
harmonious effect which others prefer. We can achieve what we
feel is a wonderful sense of movement by the use of flowing lines
of contrasting colour, whilst on the other hand, by avoiding strong
contrast in colour and long, sweeping lines, we may create a design
which will please us more by appearing quiet and completely
static.

The choice of colour is, therefore, a very personal matter, and,
although various colour theories have been put forward, suggesting
ways in which colour may best be used, the final choice of a colour
scheme will always depend very largely upon the personality of
the individual. We decide for ourselves the effect we wish to
achieve and choose a colour scheme which we think will realize
this aim. Everyone should be prepared to experiment and, from
time to time, try unusual arrangements of colour, in order to arrive
at a new effect. Each new piece of work calls for fresh experimentation, and trying out unusual colour schemes will help an embroiderer to develop the knowledge of what can be done and to find
new colour ideas. There is always a danger that, after one piece of
work has been successfully completed, a lack of experimentation
with subsequent pieces may cause both designs and colour schemes
to become repetitive.

A statement of the basic principles of colour mixing and colour
juxtaposition may be appropriate at this point for those who have
not already a good knowledge of colour.

*'Vortex Luminis'. This design,
which was worked entirely in
tent stitch on a carefully shaded
background of mosaic stitch,
with long threads of lurex and
silver couched down to give a
glittering surface effect,
suggests a swirling spiral of
light.*

There are three primary colours, red, yellow and blue, from which all the other colours are made. When two of the primary colours are mixed together, the secondary colours are obtained: red and blue when mixed together give purple; red and yellow give orange; blue and yellow give green. When two of the secondary colours are mixed together, the tertiary colours are obtained: orange and green give citron; purple and green give olive; orange and purple give russet. Each of the secondary colours also forms the complementary colour to one of the primary colours: purple is the complementary colour to yellow, green to red and orange to blue. When the primary colours are mixed with their corresponding complementary colours a neutral grey-black will result, but, if a primary colour and its complementary are placed side by side, each colour is intensified to greater brilliance.

The fact that colours vary in quality according to the nature of the other colours placed beside them is very important for the embroidery designer to bear in mind. The effects of this phenomenon can be tested by placing colours side by side and observing them, but a safe guide to work by is that relative changes in the appearance of colours when placed side by side are brought about by the influence of the after-image of one colour upon the other. An after-image is the faint coloured image seen, if, after looking intently at an area of colour for some minutes, the gaze is suddenly turned to an area of plain white. The after-image is always the complementary colour to the one first looked at, and this explains why, when complementary colours are placed side by side, it causes these colours to be intensified. A similar explanation

This detail of the 'Chloe' panel shown in full on page 97, shows the long background stitches which are worked in coton perle contrasted with the sumptuous confusion of the rhodes, smyrna, cross and tent stitches of the centre.

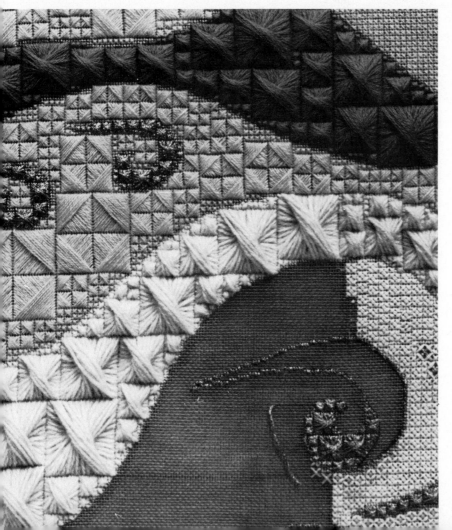

Detail of 'Seashore' panel, shown in colour on pages 2–3. This is a very satisfying piece of canvas work. The choice of stitchery fits perfectly the flowing lines of the design.

'Fluted glass'. A clever combination of colours has been used here to suggest Christmas balloons seen through reeded or fluted glass. △

'Springtime'. A patchwork of somewhat unusual pastel colouring, this panel suggests the freshness of Spring. ▷▷

This detail of 'Springtime' shows clearly the technical perfection of the stitchery. ▷

48

'Two to Five'. Three separate units of canvas work with very rich colouring and texture, which can be arranged effectively in various different groupings.

An alternative arrangement of 'Two to Five'.

Yet another arrangement of 'Two to Five'.

50

accounts for the fact that, if a strong green is placed beside a neutral grey, the grey will appear reddish, and, if a strong red is placed beside it, the grey will acquire a greenish tinge. A pale yellow placed beside red will likewise cause the latter to seem richer and purple will cause it to seem paler.

The relative brightness of colours when placed side by side can also create a sense that one area of colour, the brighter-seeming one, is nearer to the viewer than is the duller one. It is, therefore, necessary to consider this fact carefully, when building up a colour scheme for a piece of embroidery, and to decide by experiment which arrangement of colours best suits a particular design.

If it seems necessary to retain as far as possible the characteristic effect of certain colours, they can be isolated from proximity to other colours by surrounding them with an area of black or white, as these have a neutralizing effect and merely cause a change of tone, when placed beside another colour. Black causes the colour it surrounds to seem lighter and white causes it to seem darker but one must remember than an area of colour surrounded by black will appear larger than a similar area of the same colour surrounded by white.

With these few basic principles of colour in mind, the embroiderer must proceed largely by experimenting. It is almost impossible to plan in advance the exact colouring to be used for a new design: the basic colour scheme can be chosen, but from time to time as the work proceeds it will almost certainly be necessary to alter part of the original choice of colours, especially as regard to tone. Sometimes the whole appearance of a piece of work can be ruined by the choice of one wrong colour, and it may, therefore, occasionally prove necessary even to unpick a certain area of colour already worked and to replace it with something more suitable. This should not be regarded as an operation to be avoided at all costs, as it may well result in bringing to life an otherwise rather dull piece of work.

If a wall-hanging is being worked, the embroiderer should prop it up against the wall from time to time to allow it to be viewed from a distance, as it will be when it is completed. This will sometimes show the worker that a change in the chosen colour scheme is required, as the effect of the colours already used, when seen from a distance, may be quite different from what it seemed at close quarters during the actual working.

In this connection it should also be borne in mind that one should endeavour, when doing a piece of canvas work which will be viewed from a distance, to keep the colouring bright. The colours will fade eventually with the years, and this fact should be allowed for when choosing a colour scheme. It should also be remembered that the yarns in the skein always appear brighter than they do when worked on the canvas.

Texture

Whilst fully realizing the immense importance of allowing for the effects of tonal relationship between colours and the variations which this can introduce into a chosen design and colour scheme, one must also be aware of the effect which variations in the types of stitches used can bring to the texture of a piece of canvas embroidery. It is the use of a variety of stitches to interpret a design which gives canvas embroidery its true character. Stitches

'Walnut abstract'. This design was suggested as a result of examining the inner partition of the walnut shell. The starkness of the gold leather has been successfully broken by the introduction of jewels. These were securely stitched on and outlined with metallized thread and are fully integrated into the background. The large stitches on the left act as a balance to the bold mass of the gold leather and jewels on the right. ◁

Detail of 'Skeleton shell', shown in full on page 26. This mixture of french knots and beads, tightly massed in the centre of the shell, not only gives a raised texture, but it also provides a strong contrast to the smoothness of the gold leather. ▽

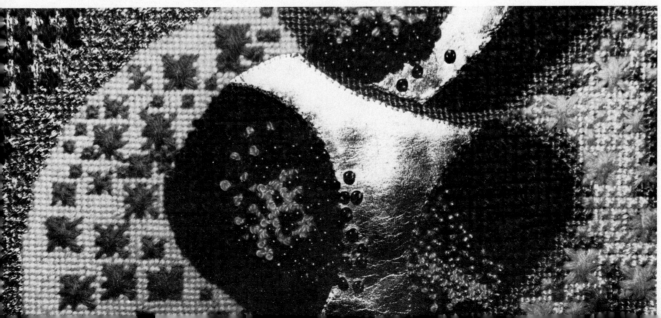

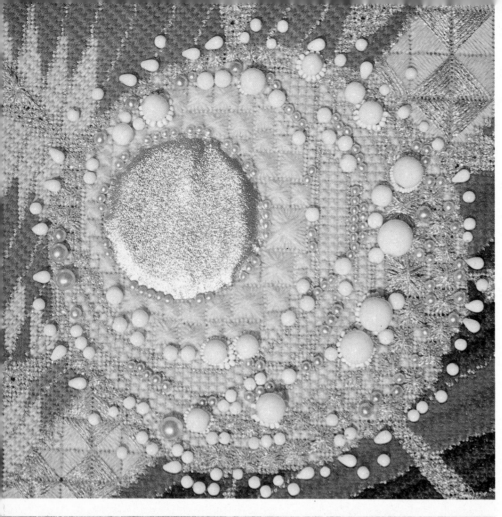

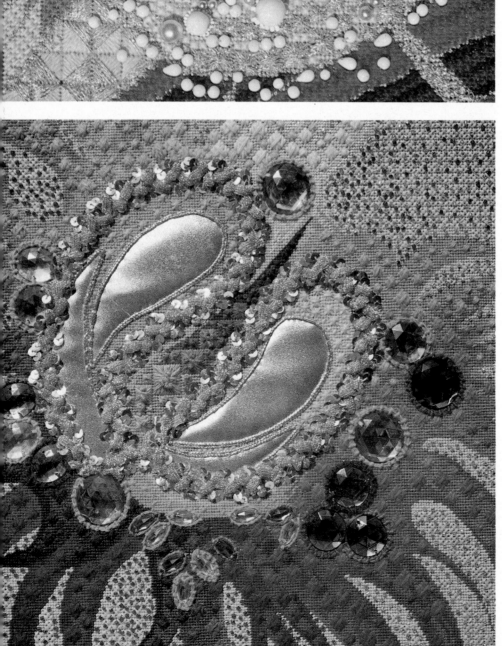

Colouring, texture and stitchery in this beautiful panel are excellent. The gold leather has been slightly padded and its smooth, shiny surface forms a pleasant contrast to the stitches worked in wool. The jewels have been carefully integrated into the design. ◁

'Gold Cross'. A very striking
design with a wonderful
combination of colour and
textural effects. The detail
shows clearly the effects of using
metallized thread, gold leather,
pearls and white china beads.

not only give texture to the design, and therefore added interest, but they can also change the tone of a colour. When areas of colour on a wall panel for instance are worked in large, raised stitches which cast shadows when the work is hung in a side-light, considerable tonal variation can occur.

In canvas work, if embroiderers strive always to preserve the special attributes of this craft and never try to work a design on canvas so that it resembles a painting, the best results will be achieved. This is the reason why I object so much to the many pre-prepared canvases based on well-known paintings, because they are too limiting and leave the worker no opportunity to develop the technique of the craft to the full. On the other hand, I do not favour an indiscriminate use of a great variety of stitches just for their own sake, but believe that it is necessary to limit the use of a particular stitch to that part of a design where it can be most effective.

The combination of stitches to achieve the best possible interpretation of a design by giving an interesting variation of texture and also retaining the beauty of the original line is the ideal. Some

'Jungle panel'. This detail from a large panel shows a clever use of stitches to give texture. The bird's wings and crest are worked in stem stitch, which is a very happy choice for the purpose.

'Old Nuremberg'. A detail of a partly-worked panel, showing how to treat buildings in a decorative rather than a realistic manner by means of attractive colour and a contrast of texture.

54

'Copper-brown panel'. A detail of a large panel which shows a wide variety of freely worked stitches, giving excellent texture.

'String panel'. This panel, which achieves good textural qualities, is worked mainly in different coloured strings on hessian. The string has been couched down and interspersed in places with canvas stitches in wool and stranded cotton. ▽

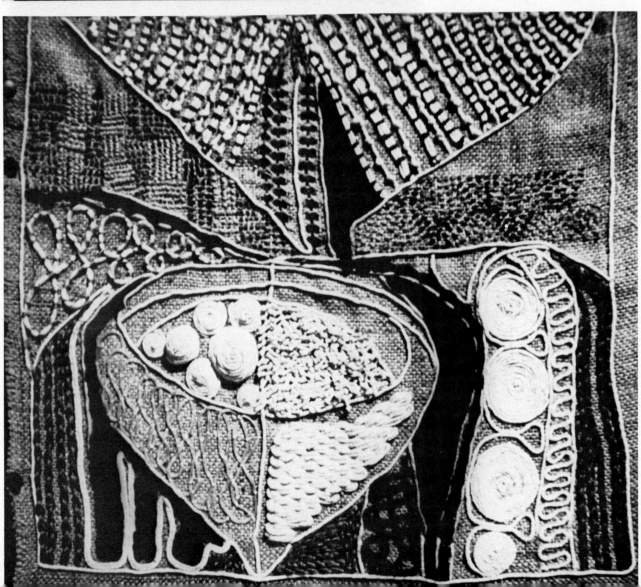

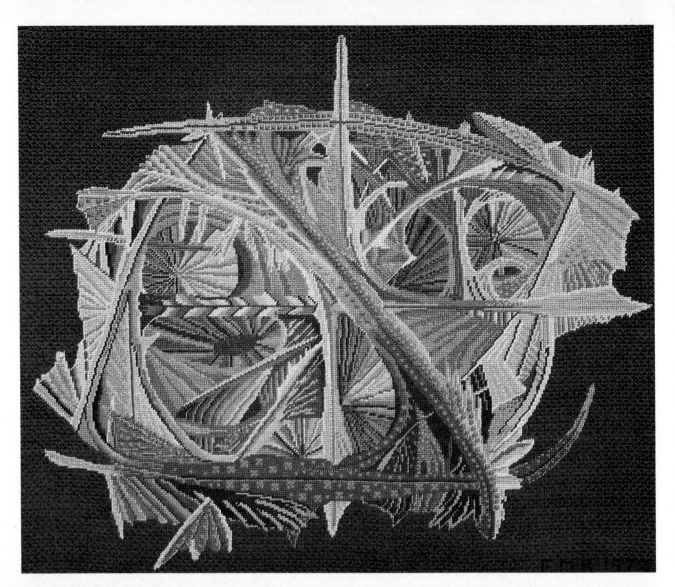

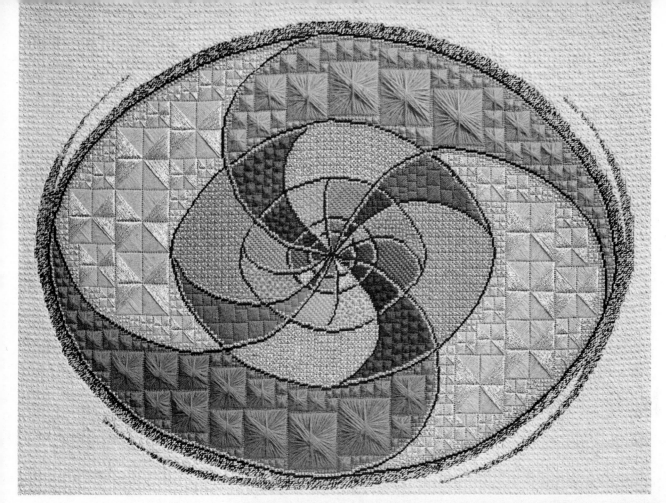

'Blue Oval'. The beautifully simple lines of this design are matched by the beauty and suitability of the stitches. △

'Quasar'. The sweeping curves in this panel, which have all been outlined in tent stitch, give it a sense of great movement. The application of silver leather at the bottom right-hand corner intensifies the dramatic effect. ▷

(opposite page:)
'Blue Crystal'. This panel, mainly in tent stitch on a rice stitch background, illustrates the usefulness of tent stitch in working a design with many curved lines, but incorporating some square stitches. △

'Sub-Aqua'. This is a linear design which requires tent stitch, but it nevertheless achieves certain textural effects by the clever use of shading. ◁

57

linear designs may call for the almost exclusive use of tent stitch and others, in which square stitches are used to fill areas bounded by curves, will require tent stitch to outline the curved shapes and prevent distortion of the design.

Colour and texture should be kept constantly in mind when a design for canvas work is being prepared, but anyone who is preparing a design for the very first time should not expect to produce an immediate masterpiece. With practice and patience, however, all things become easier, and there is no reason at all why a very pleasing, bright and attractive piece of work should not result, if attention has been given to the points in this chapter.

'Bird'. Suggested stitches for this design are given below. Blues, greens, yellow, mustard and a very small amount of Siamese pink would give a striking effect.

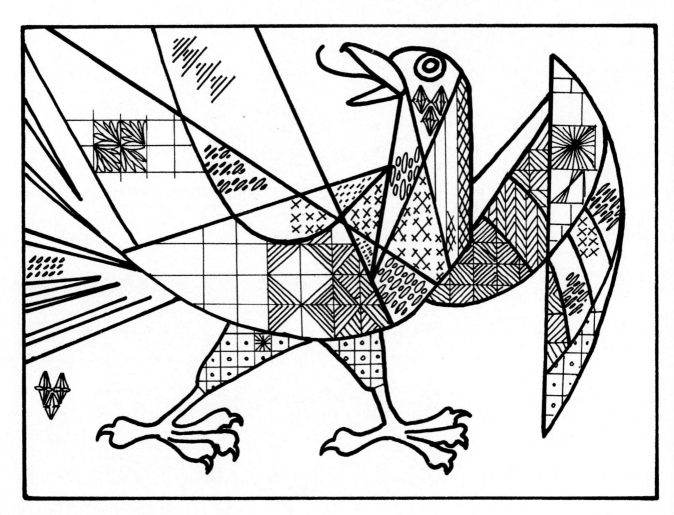

Suggestion for working:
outline everything in tent stitch
work background in small diagonal

✗ oblong cross	▨ cushion
✕ cross	▧ crossed cushion
✗✗ rice	⬚ small diagonal
⊡ eyelets	◗◖ hungarian
✦ rococo	✳ rhodes
◣ fan	⫽ milanese
⫰ mosaic	◈ french

4 Stitchery and stitch patterns

In the past, canvas work was often limited to the use of a few individual stitches only, the designs being of a kind to require working in one of the smaller stitches, such as tent stitch, which could easily render the frequent changes of colour and indicate the effects of shading. Modern designs allow the embroiderer much greater freedom, and, therefore, a greater repertory of stitches is needed now than would formerly have been necessary.

Tent stitch

Tent stitch, or petit point, is probably still the most important of all canvas stitches. Apart from back stitch, it is the smallest stitch which it is possible to use on canvas, and it is ideal for outlining parts of a design, for rendering intricate shading and for filling in small, unworked areas left after square stitches have been used.

The fact that tent stitch is small and goes into every hole of the canvas mesh makes a piece of work on which it is used very strong and durable. It is, therefore, a highly suitable stitch for working furniture coverings. It is not, however, the ideal stitch to use for working wide areas of plain ground in one colour, whether in the design or in the background. When tent stitch is used for this latter purpose, then it should be remembered that it will create a very flat effect, unless it is shaded in some way.

There are two ways in which tent stitch is often worked, but only one of these is correct for canvas work. This is shown in the diagram and involves working a stitch on the reverse of the work, like a back stitch, which is twice the size of the tent stitch on the front. The other way of working this stitch is that employed for working it on linen. This is the wrong method for working the stitch on canvas, although the result appears at first sight to be correct, when viewed from the front of the work, because it only has a tiny stitch on the reverse side, which leaves the canvas threads clearly visible. The extra wool left on the back of the work, when the correct method of working tent stitch is used, makes the wearing properties of the finished work greater and gives it a much fuller appearance.

Reversed tent stitch △

Tent stitch ▽

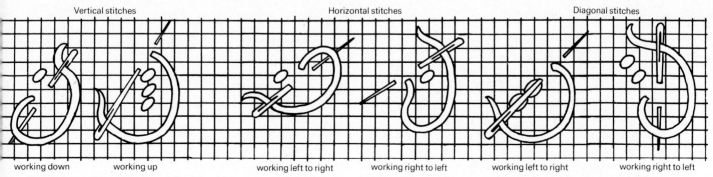

Vertical stitches		Horizontal stitches		Diagonal stitches	
working down	working up	working left to right	working right to left	working left to right	working right to left

'Red Goat'. This panel not only shows a richness of colour and texture, but also demonstrates how a certain amount of distortion in the subject of the design can bring originality to a piece of work.

60

This detail of 'Sub Aqua', shown in full on page 56, shows the effective use of tent stitch. ◁

'Sea Spirit', a partly worked panel. The powerful design suggesting the turbulence of the sea, depends entirely on the imaginative use of colour and stitchery. ▽

Florentine stitch △▽

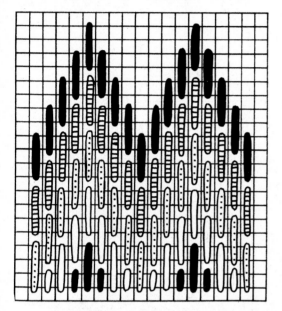

Florentine pattern ▽

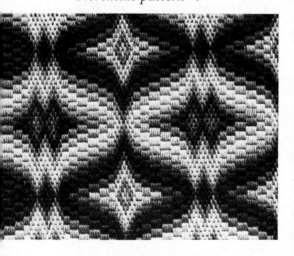

Algerian stitch ▷

Florentine stitch

One of the most popular stitches, with beginners, is one which has been in constant use over a very long period, florentine stitch or flame stitch, also known as Bargello work. Originally the name florentine stitch covered a large group of straight and diagonal stitches, such as cushion, mosaic, hungarian and several other straight stitches, but later these stitches were sub-divided and only the straight stitch patterns which form the familiar shape of zig-zag or flame retain the original name.

This stitch is perhaps the easiest of all the canvas stitches to work. It is exceedingly quick to do, and this fact probably explains its popularity with beginners and the reason why so many hangings and other furnishings have been worked in this stitch over the last few centuries. Florentine stitch also makes a very good covering for furniture, provided the wool used is of the correct thickness to cover the canvas comfortably. This point is important to watch, as florentine is a straight stitch which is worked only over the horizontal threads of the canvas, the wool in each stitch going up between two vertical threads, and on no account should any of the canvas threads be visible on the surface of the completed work. If, therefore, thin crewel wool is used, exactly the right number of threads must be taken in the needle to cover the canvas adequately. The only way of assessing the correct number of strands to use is by working a few stitches and testing the effect, as the wool in the needle must not be thicker than will go comfortably through the mesh of the canvas. If the wool is too thick, it will distort the threads of the canvas and will also make working very difficult.

Algerian stitch

Algerian stitch consists of eight individual stitches worked over four vertical and four horizontal threads of the canvas. The needle is brought up from the back to the front of the canvas at point A in the diagram, taken over two threads diagonally and down into the centre hole B. The work continues in this way around the centre with the working thread always coming from the outside edge of the stitch and down into the centre hole. A sharp tug should be given to the thread each time in order to emphasize the centre hole which is a feature of this stitch.

If wool is used for working algerian stitch, it should be of a fine or medium thickness in order to keep the centre hole clear, but silk, pearl cotton (coton perle or Sylko), stranded cotton or coton a broder are preferable, because of their greater pulling power.

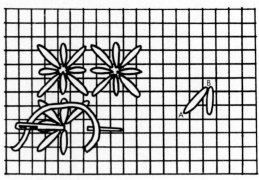

Algerian stitch

Bullion stitch

The following is the method for working bullion stitch on canvas on a frame, see diagram A. (For method of working this stitch in the hand, see diagram B.) Bring the working thread up from the back of the canvas at a spot where one end of the bullion knot is to be made, A. Insert the needle the required length of the stitch further back to the right at B, and leave the working thread as loose as possible on the surface of the canvas. Bring the tip of the needle up again through the canvas at A, and hold the needle in a vertical position with the left hand under the canvas, whilst the working thread is taken between the thumb and first finger of the right hand and wrapped several times around the tip of the needle, the number of times depending upon the length of the stitch to be worked. Bring the left hand up to the surface and hold the coil of thread close to the canvas with thumb and forefinger. With the right hand gently ease the needle through the canvas and the coil. Now pull in the opposite direction, so that the coil lies flat in its proper position on the canvas. Tighten the working thread by pulling it and take the needle down through the canvas again at B.

Bullion stitch

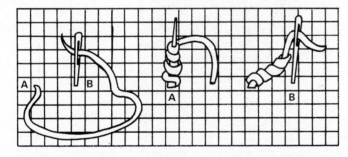

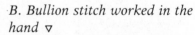

A. Bullion stitch worked on a frame ◁

B. Bullion stitch worked in the hand ▽

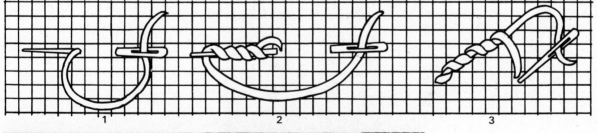

Long bullion stitch worked over diamond satin stitch ◁

63

'Morning Light'. This example of colour gradation creates the effect of light shining through a stained-glass window. The design could be considered as a kind of modern canvas work sampler.

'Lute'. The basic lines of this design, which is worked in tent stitch on a rice-stitch background, are extremely simple. The colouring is deep and rich with a central area of brilliance, which makes the panel so strikingly satisfying. Large and small sequins, together with silver thread couched down in places, give a certain lightness to the whole design. Some of the radiating lines are worked in silver metallic threads in tent stitch while others are couched silver threads. Three very large sequins are stitched down at the point where the lines converge.

Buttonhole stitch

This is a good stitch for 'oversewing' the turned-in edge of the canvas when a hole is cut.

Buttonhole stitch worked over bars. △

Buttonhole stitch used to edge a hole cut in the canvas. △

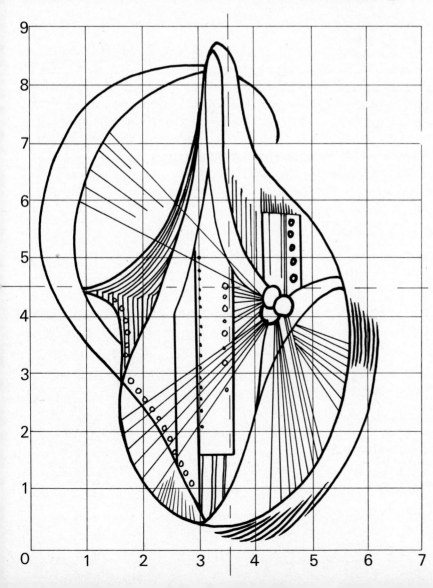

Enlarge this diagram to work the panel 'Lute', shown on facing page. ◁

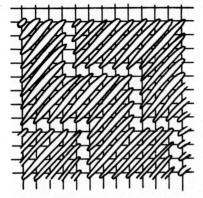

Byzantine stitch △ ▷

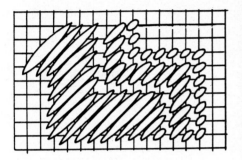

Jacquard stitch, a variation of byzantine stitch

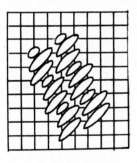

Cashmere stitch

Byzantine stitch

This stitch is worked diagonally across four or more vertical and horizontal threads of the canvas in a series of 'steps'. There is a variation of this stitch in which the size of the stitches in adjacent rows of 'steps' may differ. This is sometimes called *Jacquard stitch*.

Cashmere stitch

This is a useful stitch for covering large areas of background. It consists of three diagonal stitches, one over a single intersection of the canvas, followed by two over two intersections. The three stitches of each unit start immediately beneath one another and are worked from left to right. Each unit of three begins one hole to the right of the point where the last stitch in the first unit was commenced. Succeeding rows of stitches fit snugly into the spaces left by the row before them, but the exact positioning of individual stitches is best seen by consulting the diagram.

Chequer stitch

This stitch pattern is formed by alternating cushion stitch (page 68) with a square of tent stitch (page 59).

Chequer stitch ▷

Cross stitch

Cross stitch, like tent stitch, is one of the basic canvas work stitches. It was very popular in the late nineteenth century, but has now lost some of its popularity. Cross stitch forms a tiny cross and is worked by taking the yarn diagonally over two horizontal and two vertical threads of the canvas. Each cross should be completed before passing on to the next, and all the uppermost stitches on each cross should pass in the same direction.

The method of working cross stitch as shown in the diagram is the most suitable for canvas work, as it leaves more yarn on the underside than does the method of working generally used on linen. This makes for great durability, which is very necessary when furniture coverings are being worked.

In the past it was usual to work cross stitch in rows horizontally, vertically or diagonally across the canvas, but now it is also used to follow the line of the design, whether it is straight or curved, and in the form of single stitches dotted all over an area to give texture.

A variant of cross stitch, which may be called oblong cross stitch, can be worked over one vertical and several horizontal threads of the canvas.

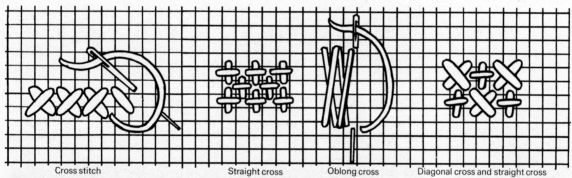

Cross stitch   Straight cross   Oblong cross   Diagonal cross and straight cross

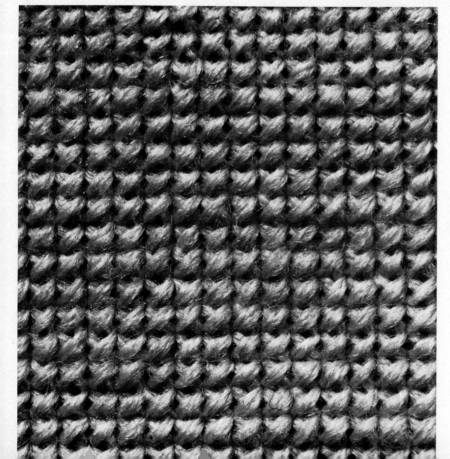

Oblong cross stitch △

Cross stitch ◁

67

Cushion or Scottish stitch

This is a square stitch in which a set of five individual diagonal stitches is worked over a sequence of one, two, three, two and one intersections of the canvas. The cushions are worked in rows horizontally, and each cushion is generally completely surrounded by a row of tent stitch, but this can be omitted, in which case the stitches of the second cushion will start from the same holes in the canvas into which those of the first cushion were worked.

There are several variations of this stitch, each bearing a different name. When the cushions are placed in rows diagonally, for instance, and the rows are separated from one another by single rows of tent stitch, it is called *Moorish stitch*.

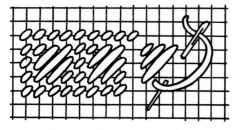

Cushion stitch △ ▷

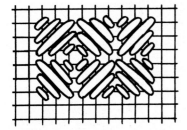

Cushion stitch variation △

Cushion stitch without tent stitch ▷

Crossed cushion stitch ▷

Diagonal stitch (large and small)

This is another good stitch for filling large areas of background.
Large diagonal stitch. In this larger form, the stitch consists of four stitches taken diagonally over two, three, four and three intersections of the canvas respectively, working from top left to bottom right, and repeating that sequence. Subsequent rows of the stitch fit into the line of stitches in the previous row, the largest stitch always coming in line diagonally with the smallest one in the previous row.

Small diagonal stitch consists of one diagonal stitch over one intersection of the canvas, followed by one over two intersections, or, in other words, one tent stitch (petit point) followed by one large tent stitch (gros point) repeated indefinitely along a diagonal from top left to bottom right, with subsequent rows fitting in beside one another.

Small diagonal stitch △

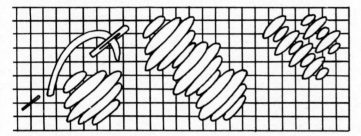

Large diagonal stitch △   *Small diagonal stitch* △

Large diagonal stitch ◁

Diamond straight stitch ▽

Diamond Straight stitch

The basic element in this stitch is a diamond shape formed by placing side by side five upright straight stitches which pass over one, three, five, three and one horizontal threads of the canvas respectively. The outer part of the diamond shape is completed by working a row of small, upright stitches all round, each passing over one horizontal thread of the canvas. A photograph of this stitch in use will be seen on page 113, where it appears as the background stitch on the finger plate shown on the left-hand side.

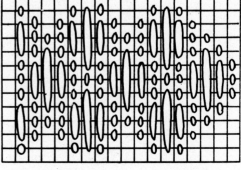

69

Double knot stitch △

Double knot stitch worked in raffene △

Eyelet stitch ▽

Double Knot stitch

This stitch should be started with a twisted chain stitch as shown at A in the diagram. The needle is then taken under the base of the chain stitch from right to left (B), and the yarn is brought right round the base of stitch (C), under the lower layer of the twisted chain and over its upper layer. Once more the yarn is taken right round the stitch, and the needle is put into the canvas just one hole to the left of where the initial stitch began. The needle should be brought out again at the base of the stitch and through the final loop formed (D). The second stitch is immediately started off with another twisted chain stitch.

This double knot stitch can be worked either as a continuous line of stitches or as separate units.

Double knot stitch

Eyelet stitch

This stitch is similar to algerian stitch, page 62, except that the individual stitches are worked from every hole around the perimeter into the centre hole. It can be worked over any number of threads of the canvas from one up to the largest number which will leave the centre hole clearly visible. Eyelet stitch is generally worked as a square stitch, but it can be worked as a diamond shape as well.

Eyelet stitch

Eyelet with satin stitch

Diamond eyelet stitch

Fan stitch or Ray stitch

This square stitch is generally worked to cover an area of three vertical and three horizontal threads of the canvas. Seven straight stitches fan out from one corner of the square into the holes along the opposite two sides. The stitch can be varied by working alternate horizontal rows with the stitches radiating from opposite corners of the square.

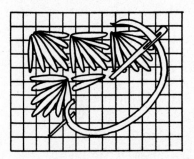

Fan stitch △▽

Fan stitch used in background with italian two-sided stitch

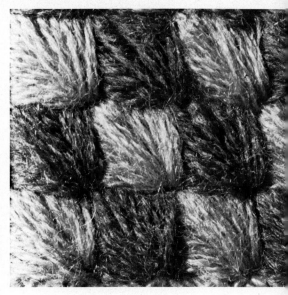

Fern stitch

To work fern stitch the needle is brought up at A, as shown in the diagram, taken to the right and down over two intersections of the canvas, under the vertical thread from right to left and up to the right over two intersections. The needle is then taken down behind the first stitch and brought out three vertical threads of the canvas to the left and one horizontal thread down, so that it emerges immediately beneath the first stitch. This process is repeated, each row of stitches being commenced at the top and worked down.

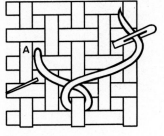

Fern stitch

71

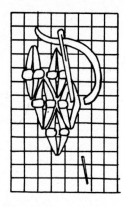

French stitch △▽

French stitch

This stitch is generally worked diagonally across the canvas, but it can be worked horizontally to give the same effect.

A vertical stitch is first worked over four horizontal threads of the canvas, and the needle is brought out two threads down and one to the left of the first stitch. A small horizontal stitch is now taken to the right over one canvas thread and the first stitch. The needle is brought out in the same hole as the beginning of the first stitch, and a similar vertical stitch is put in beside the first one, the needle entering the same hole at the top. Finally, the needle is brought out two threads down and one to the right of the second vertical stitch and inserted in the centre hole between the two stitches, thus tying the second one down.

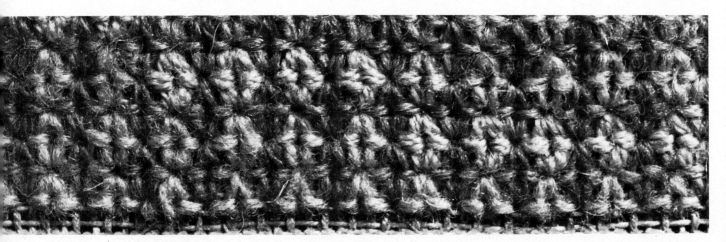

French knots

For this stitch the yarn should be brought up through the canvas at the exact spot where the knot is required and should be held firmly between the thumb and first finger of the left hand, whilst the needle is twisted once or twice around it. The twists of yarn should be tightened on the needle, the point of which should then be turned away from the worker and inserted over one intersection of the canvas. It could really be described almost as a knotted tent stitch.

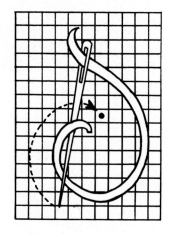

French knots △▷

French knots with tent stitch

Ghiordes Knot, for use in Turkey Work

This stitch is started from the front of the canvas and is worked from the bottom left-hand corner of the area to be covered. The loose end of the yarn is held between forefinger and thumb of the left hand, while the needle is taken under one vertical thread of the canvas from right to left. Then with the working thread held loosely, put the needle under the next vertical thread of the canvas to the right and, again moving it from right to left, bring it up through the same hole in the canvas where the first stitch was started in such a way that the needle passes under the loop of the working thread. Tighten this loop by pulling the two ends of the yarn down firmly. Repeat the process under the next vertical thread of the canvas to the right, whilst at the same time holding down a loop of the yarn with your thumb, and continue thus until a whole row of stitches has been completed. Cut the working thread at the end of the row and begin the next row on the left two threads of the canvas above and one thread to the right of the first stitch in the first row, so that the rows of stitches will be staggered. Finally, the loops can be cut and trimmed to form a pile (approximate depth $\frac{1}{4}$ inch).

Gobelin stitch

The name Gobelin covers a whole group of straight satin stitches, which can be used to form a variety of interesting stitch patterns as shown in the illustrations.

To work the basic form of this stitch proceed in horizontal rows from top to bottom of the area of canvas to be covered, the first row being put in from left to right, the second from right to left, and so on. Start by bringing the needle up through the canvas and take a diagonal stitch downwards across two horizontal intersections and one vertical thread to the left. Bring the needle

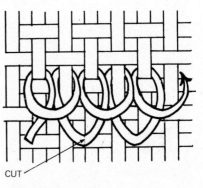

CUT

Ghiordes knot △

Gobelin stitch worked in various widths (1)

Gobelin stitch encroaching (2)

2

1

Gobelin stitch. Blocks of satin stitch have been worked here with some tent stitches between them (1)

Gobelin stitch alternating with cross stitch and forming an attractive flower pattern (2)

up again to the surface two horizontal threads up and two vertical threads to the right and continue working in this way until the row is finished. The next row is worked from right to left, but this time the needle is brought up through the canvas two horizontal threads below and one vertical thread to the left of the point where the last stitch in the first row had begun and is taken down again through the canvas into the hole where this last stitch had begun. The remaining stitches in this row are put in in the same way beneath the corresponding stitches in the first row.

1

4

3

2

Gobelin stitch variation. Oval-shaped blocks of satin stitch have been used here (3)

Gobelin stitch forming a half-drop pattern with tent stitch (4)

Hungarian stitch

This is an attractive stitch which is useful for shading a large area, as it can be worked either in one colour or in rows of contrasting colours. It consists of three upright straight stitches, worked over two, four and two horizontal threads of the canvas respectively. Two vertical threads of the canvas, or one hole, are left uncovered between each group of three stitches, so that the long stitches of the following row can be worked into the space, and the rows are thus interlocked.

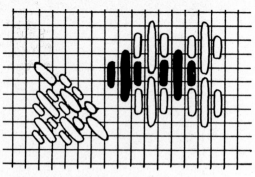

Hungarian stitch ◁ △

Interlocking Leaf stitch

This charming stitch is new and was evolved by working a row of leaf stitch, page 76, and then reversing it for the second row, thus forming a continuous flowing line of stitches. The detail below is from the piece of work, shown on pages 2–3, on which it was first used. It has proved an excellent stitch for working a curved line and offers scope for further experimentation.

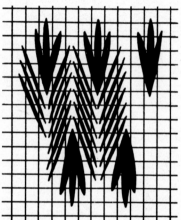

Interlocking leaf stitch ◁ △

Italian Two-sided stitch

This is a useful background stitch, the working of which needs little or no explanation, as the diagram plainly shows the four stages in its construction (see also photograph on following page).

Italian two-sided stitch

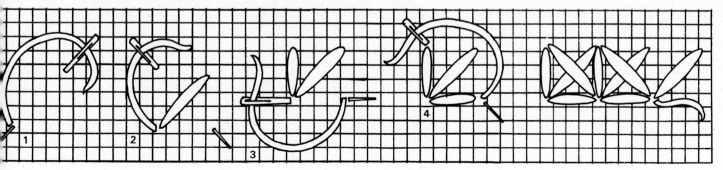

Italian two-sided stitch

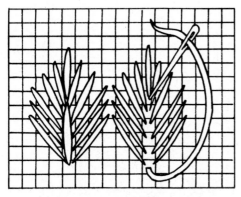

Leaf stitch

A variation of leaf stitch shown with interlocking leaf stitch.

Jacquard stitch

See byzantine stitch, page 66.

Leaf stitch

This stitch starts with a vertical straight stitch down over four threads of the canvas. Then two stitches are put in, each over four threads, one starting one thread down and one thread to the right, and the other one thread down and one thread to the left of the point where the first stitch started, and both finishing in the hole immediately below where the first stitch ended. The next stitch starts another one thread down and one thread further to the left and is taken down into the hole in the canvas immediately beneath the previous stitch. This is followed by three stitches of the same length, each placed one horizontal thread of the canvas lower than the one before and lying parallel to it. The other side of the leaf stitch is completed in the same way. The final stitch down the centre of the leaf, as shown in the diagram, is optional.

The leaf shape can be made wider or narrower by varying the number of threads of the canvas covered by single stitches.

Long-legged Cross stitch

Commence this stitch by bringing up the needle through the canvas at the point marked A on the diagram. Take the yarn over four horizontal and four vertical threads of the canvas into hole B, and bring the needle out again four threads below this point at C. The yarn is then taken obliquely forward over four horizontal and eight vertical canvas threads to D, and the needle is brought out four threads down, ready to commence another stitch. The process is then repeated to make subsequent stitches.

The depth of this stitch can be varied and it can be worked over two, four or six horizontal threads of the canvas.

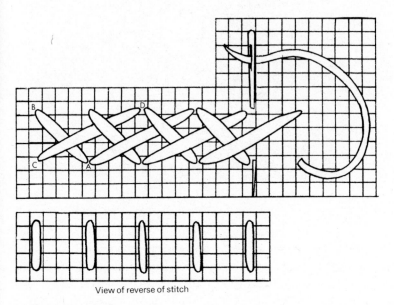

View of reverse of stitch

Milanese stitch

This attractive stitch is worked in rows diagonally across the canvas, generally from top left to bottom right. It consists of four individual stitches taken diagonally first over one intersection of the canvas, then over two, three and four intersections to form a small triangular shape. The working of these shapes continues along the diagonal, and then the next row of triangles is put in in reverse, so that they fit exactly together with the first row, as shown in the diagram, the longest stitch in one triangle always coming next to the shortest in the next.

This stitch can also be worked as a series of back stitches proceeding diagonally from bottom left to top right of the canvas. The first row consists of stitches taken alternately over one and four intersections of the canvas; the second row passes alternately over two and three intersections; the third over three and two and the fourth over four and one. The whole process is then repeated.

Long-legged cross stitch ◁ △

Milanese with satin stitch △

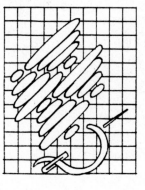

Milanese stitch ◁ △

Moorish stitch

See cushion stitch, page 68.

Mosaic stitch

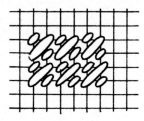

Mosaic stitch △▽

This is a neat and attractive square stitch which, when worked, closely resembles in effect a small cross stitch. It is useful for backgrounds and can be successfully employed for shading. Each stitch consists of a group of three diagonal stitches worked over two horizontal and two vertical threads of the canvas, the first stitch over one intersection of the canvas, the second over two intersections and the third over one. It is, in fact, two normal tent stitches with one large tent stitch over two threads in between them.

Mosaic stitch is used to work the faces in this panel with stem stitch for the hair ▷

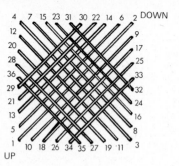

Norwich stitch ◁ △

Norwich stitch

This stitch is best when worked with a tightly spun wool such as nylon knitting wool or coton perle. It may be worked in various sizes, provided it is a square with an uneven number of threads of the canvas. The diagram shows the stitches in order of working. It will be noticed that the method of working follows a regular pattern until the last stitch is put in, when the needle is slipped under instead of over stitch 29–30, the last stitch it passes before entering the canvas at hole 36.

Parisian stitch

This is a vertical straight stitch similar to hungarian stitch, page 74, but it is worked over two and four horizontal threads of the canvas only, this sequence being repeated indefinitely with no threads of canvas left uncovered between the groups of two vertical stitches.

Parisian stitch △

Variation of Parisian stitch △

Parisian stitch worked in cotton thread ◁

79

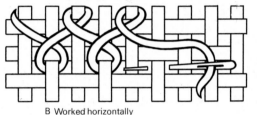

A Worked vertically

B Worked horizontally

Plaited stitch △ ▷

Plaited stitch

This stitch is similar to fern stitch, page 71, except that the vertical rows of stitches overlap one another by one thread of canvas and thus give to the finished work a closely interwoven appearance rather like knitting.

As shown in the diagram, it is also possible to work this stitch in rows horizontally.

Portuguese Stem stitch

This stitch is normally worked on linen, but it can also be used quite successfully on canvas. It is a very useful stitch where a knotted, slightly raised line is needed.

The working of the stitch is completed in three movements. Start with an ordinary stem stitch, worked over one vertical and four horizontal threads of the canvas, bringing the needle out two threads down and one to the left, as shown at A in the diagram. The needle is then slipped under the first stitch from right to left, as at B, and the yarn is wrapped round the stitch and tightened. The process of wrapping the yarn round the stitch is then repeated, keeping the second coil just below the first (C).

A second stitch is put in by entering the needle two horizontal threads of the canvas beyond the end of the first stitch and bringing it out again two threads back on the left of the first stitch (D). The needle is now taken under the top part of the first stitch and the bottom part of the second stitch, and the yarn is wrapped round the stitch as before to make two coils, one beneath the other (E).

Portuguese stem stitch △▽

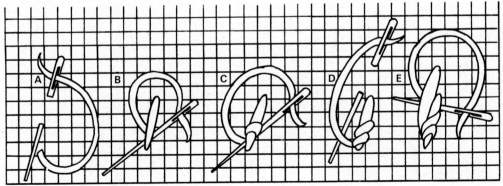

Rhodes stitch (detail from 'Seashore', pages 2–3) ▷

Rhodes stitch

This stitch was thought up when an extra large, bulky stitch was needed for working a particular canvas work panel, and it has proved a very useful and attractive addition to an already long list of stitches. It is a square stitch which may be worked over any area of the canvas from a minimum of three horizontal by three vertical threads. If a smaller stitch than this is required for use in conjunction with a group of rhodes stitches, then smyrna stitch can be successfully employed.

The stitch is worked by starting with an individual diagonal stitch running from one corner to the other of the chosen square. The work then continues around the square, moving always in one direction, until a stitch which passes across the centre of the area has been worked into every hole around the edge of the square, see diagram A. The continued overlapping of the yarn in the centre of the stitch builds up to give a very high, raised effect, which somewhat resembles a rather flat pyramid when viewed from the side.

If the stitch to be worked is very large, as, for instance, one covering twenty-four horizontal threads of the canvas, then a long stitch can be taken across the corners of the completed rhodes stitch to hold it down, or a small stitch can tie it down in the centre, see diagram B. Such extra stitches, when taken across the corners, can only be introduced successfully, however, if the large rhodes stitch covers an even number of threads of the canvas.

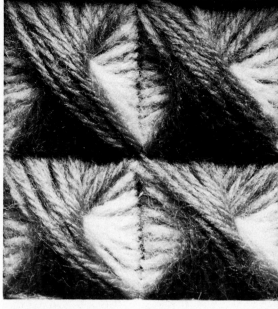

Rhodes stitch in two colours △

Combination of half a rhodes stitch with satin stitch ▽

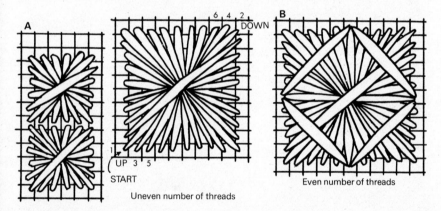

Rhodes stitch △

Rice stitch or Crossed Corners

This square stitch is begun by working a large diagonal cross stitch over an even number of threads of the canvas. The needle is then brought up through the hole in the centre of the side of the cross, and a back stitch is taken across the arm of the cross and down into the centre hole on the top edge of it. The needle is then again brought up through the centre hole opposite on the bottom edge of the cross stitch, and another small stitch is taken across an arm of the cross and down into the same hole where the first small stitch started. Once more the needle is brought up, but this time at the centre hole on the opposite side of the cross stitch, and is taken back across an arm of the cross into the same hole on the bottom edge, where the second small stitch started. Finally the needle is brought up through the centre hole on the top edge of the cross stitch and across the fourth arm of the cross into the hole on the side where the third small stitch started.

In this way individual rice stitches can be worked, but, if it is desired to put in the small stitches in a contrasting colour or with a different type of yarn, then a row of the basic cross stitches should be worked first, and the small stitches should be put in afterwards.

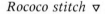

Rice stitch △ ▷

Rococo stitch ▽

Rococo stitch

This is an attractive stitch in which a group of vertical, straight stitches, even in number, is worked by passing the yarn each time through the same holes in the canvas, but tying each individual stitch in the middle to a thread of the canvas, so as to produce a balanced effect. If the stitches pass over an even number of horizontal threads of the canvas, a back stitch should be used to tie them down, but, if they pass over an uneven number of threads, a tent stitch must be used.

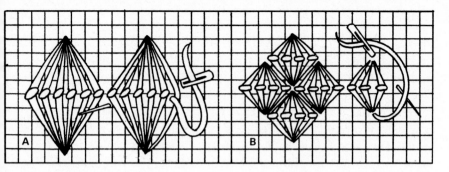

Tie down with tent stitch if the threads
are of uneven number

Tie down with back stitch if the threads
are an even number

Shell stitch

Shell stitch is worked like wheatsheaf stitch, page 85, but, as it
always passes over an even number of horizontal threads of the
canvas, it should be tied down in the centre with a back stitch and
not a tent stitch. When a row of stitches of this type has been
worked, adjacent ones are joined together by coiling the yarn
through the back stitches one and a half times.

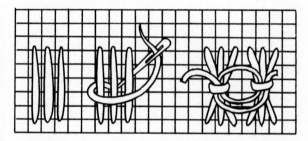

Shell stitch

Smyrna stitch

This stitch, which is sometimes known as *Leviathan* or *Double
Cross*, consists of a large diagonal cross stitch with a straight cross
worked over it. It can be worked over two, four or more even
numbers of threads of the canvas and is a very useful stitch for
working in conjunction with rhodes stitch, especially when it is
necessary to fill odd shapes. The top stitches of the straight crosses
should all be worked in one direction, either all horizontally or all
vertically.

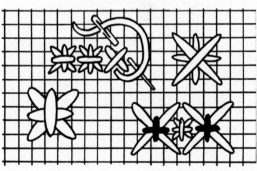

Smyrna stitch ◁ △

83

Spider's webs or wheels

A group of stitches of even length is worked radiating from a central point. The needle is then brought out one hole below the centre and to the right of the radial stitch on that side. It passes over and wraps the yarn once round this radial stitch, is taken to the right and under the next radial stitch, around which the yarn is again wrapped. This process of passing the working thread under and around each of the radial stitches in turn is continued right round the circle several times, until all the radial stitches are completely covered and form raised ridges.

There is another way of working this stitch, which does not cause ridges to form on the surface. This is to use an uneven number of stitches to form the radial lines from the central point and to weave the yarn in the needle over and under adjacent stitches all round the circle, without wrapping any of the individual stitches.

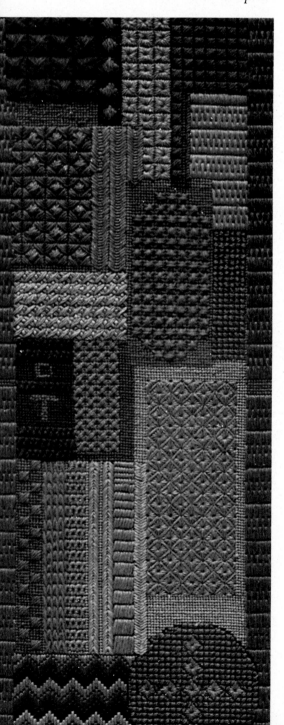

A modern canvas work sampler ▽

Spider's webs, worked with smyrna stitches over a background of cross stitch △

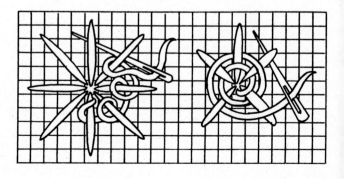

Spider's webs

Stem stitch or Outline stitch

This stitch is generally regarded as a crewel work stitch to be used solely on a silk, cotton or linen ground and is seldom seen worked as a modern canvas work stitch. It is useful, however, as an outlining stitch and will also cover the canvas well, when used as a filling stitch.

The method of working is the same as is used for crewel work: a long stitch is taken over a number of threads of the canvas, and the needle is brought out again beside this stitch and half-way back along its length, before moving forward once more. For an illustration of this stitch in use on canvas see the panel of two faces on page 78 where the hair is worked in stem stitch.

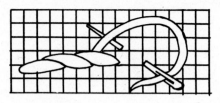

Stem stitch

Wheatsheaf stitch

This stitch consists of three straight stitches taken over four or more horizontal threads of the canvas. The needle is then brought up in the centre hole, taken out to the left, over the three stitches to the right and down again into the same hole. If the three straight stitches pass over an uneven number of threads of the canvas, they can be tied down with a tent stitch.

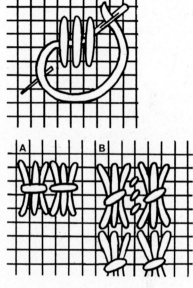

Wheatsheaf stitch △
A. *Even number of threads*
B. *Uneven number of threads*

Wheatsheaf stitch ◁

Expanding wheatsheaf stitch

5 Materials and equipment

Canvas

Basically, there are two kinds of embroidery canvas, the single-thread (Congress) canvas sometimes known as Mono and the double-thread canvas which is known as Penelope canvas. These canvases are available in a wide range of meshes, the mesh of a canvas being the number of threads to the inch, and they vary from as fine as thirty-two threads to the inch up to the coarse type of canvas used for rug-making, which has only four threads to the inch. Canvas comes in various widths, ranging from twelve inches to fifty-nine inches, and it is necessary, therefore, when purchasing canvas to state the quantity, width and mesh required: e.g. one yard of twenty-seven inch wide, 16 mesh single canvas, or if double, Penelope canvas is to be purchased, one yard of thirty-six inch wide 16/32 mesh canvas.

When deciding the correct mesh to use, it is first necessary to have a reasonably clear idea of the type of design to be worked and the fineness of the detail to be put into it. The experienced canvas embroiderer will have no difficulty in choosing the most suitable canvas for her design, but to someone starting canvas work for the first time, the range of meshes which are available can present something of a problem. If the design is to be a bold one without much detail, then one of the coarser mesh canvases can be used with either 12 or 14 threads to the inch, but for a fairly fine and detailed design, a medium canvas with 16 or 18 threads to the inch would be more suitable. I find 14 or 16 mesh usually very good for chair-seats, hassocks, stool-tops and cushions, as well as for pictures and small wall hangings, but, where very large designs are concerned, 12 mesh can prove more suitable. For articles such as evening bags, or anything with a very fine, intricate design, 18 or 20 mesh may be needed, or perhaps an even finer one.

A simple way of testing whether the mesh of a canvas is suitable for a certain design is to place the design, clearly outlined in black, under the canvas so that it can be seen through the mesh and then to make sure that it will be possible to work all the details of the design comfortably. Too coarse a canvas would make this impossible, but, nevertheless, the canvas finally chosen needs to be no finer than is necessary to ensure that the design can be worked easily and without loss of any of the original detail. There is simply no virtue in working a coarse design on a fine canvas: this would actually cause the finished piece to become insipid and to lose all of its real character, after having involved the worker in many unnecessary extra hours of work.

Use the best quality canvas that can be obtained when working furniture coverings and, although it can be either single or double-thread, I prefer the single-thread canvas, as most stitches

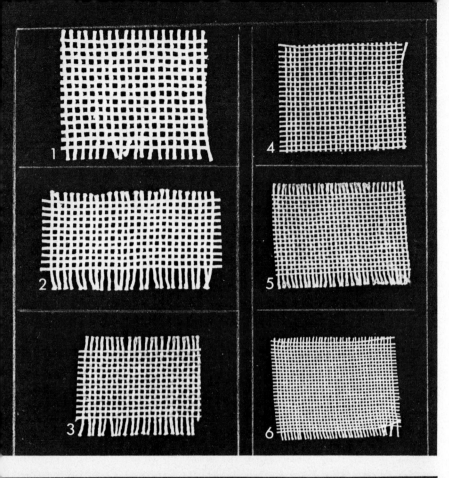

Single-thread (Congress or Mono) canvas.
1. 36 inches wide, brown &
white
7/14 threads = 1 inch
2. 36 inches wide
8/16 threads = 1 inch
3. 36 inches wide
9/18 threads = 1 inch
4. 18, 23, 26, 36, 44 & 54
inches wide
10/20 threads = 1 inch
5. 26 inches wide
11/22 threads = 1 inch
6. 26 inches wide
12/24 threads = 1 inch

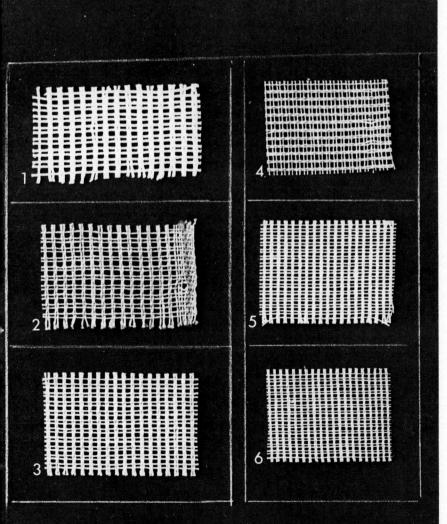

Double-thread (Penelope)
canvas.
1. 38 inches wide, white only
10 threads = 1 inch
2. 36 inches wide, brown &
white
12 threads = 1 inch
3. 26 inches wide, brown only
36 inches wide, brown & white
14 threads = 1 inch
4. 23 & 27 inches wide, brown
only
36 inches wide, brown & white
16 threads = 1 inch
5. 23, 27 & 36 inches wide,
brown only
18 threads = 1 inch
6. 22½ inches wide
24 threads = 1 inch
Also obtainable:
20 & 22 threads = 1 inch

can be worked on it without difficulty. It may perhaps be said that florentine and rococo stitches can be worked more successfully on double-thread than on single-thread canvas, but these are lesser-used stitches. The most important canvas work stitches, such as tent stitch (petit point), are much more difficult to work on double-thread canvas, as the work always necessitates splitting the double-thread, which is indeed an exceedingly tedious pastime. For wall-panels and pictures, canvas of any quality can be used.

For extremely experimental pieces, hessian is a possible alternative to canvas, and even chicken wire need not be despised as a material upon which to work stitchery.

One of the best canvases is a natural coloured, polished cotton thread canvas made in widths of twenty-seven and thirty-six inches. Cheaper cotton canvases are stocked by some large stores in buff or white. These canvases, however, unlike the more expensive ones, have been stiffened by the use of size and they become sticky, limp and stained, if they come into contact with moisture. Another type of canvas which is sometimes used for canvas embroidery is a material made from Italian hemp, which is very strong and flexible and is in some respects nearer to the material used in very early days for canvas work. It is known as Winchester canvas and is made in a width of fifty inches, which makes it particularly useful for working large panels. As this flexible canvas is easier to join together than the stiffer kind, Winchester canvas is also good for working panels where an even greater width than fifty inches is required. There is a similar type of canvas made from flax which is also fifty inches wide. When certain stitches are worked on this type of flexible canvas, the effect is quite different from what results when the same stitches are worked on the stiffer Congress canvas. This difference is caused because the pull of the stitches results in a greater displacement of the fibres of the Winchester canvas, and it is most noticeable in the working of such stitches as eyelet, diagonal, rococo and hungarian, where the small perforations appearing between stitches add greatly to the general appearance of the finished work.

Yarns

The principal yarn used in working covers for pieces of upholstered furniture and for such objects as cushions, chair squabs, bags or kneelers is undoubtedly wool, or a combination of wool with a little silk. Wool is strong and easy to work with and it gives the best possible coverage of the canvas, a most important point where furnishings are concerned. The resulting fabric is also extremely durable and has the quality of 'wearing clean', so that an article worked in wool needs no more than an occasional gentle brushing and tapping to keep it in good condition. Dry-cleaning can, however, be undertaken, if it is thought necessary.

With the exception of the very soft 'baby' wool, all kinds of wool can be used for canvas work, provided it is fine enough for the thread to be pulled through the holes in the canvas without damage. For furniture coverings, a strong two-ply Shetland wool, or other similar type such as Atherstone or Appleton, is to be preferred, but other wools, such as Anchor tapisserie, crewel wool and many knitting wools, including crepe wool, can be used,

This detail of the 'Chloe' panel, shown in full on page 97, shows the effective use of raffene and sequins with wool. The contrast is clearly seen between the close texture of the outer circle and the openness of the centre which is only sparsely covered with large cushion stitches worked in raffene and large and small smyrna stitches with sequins and beads intermingling.

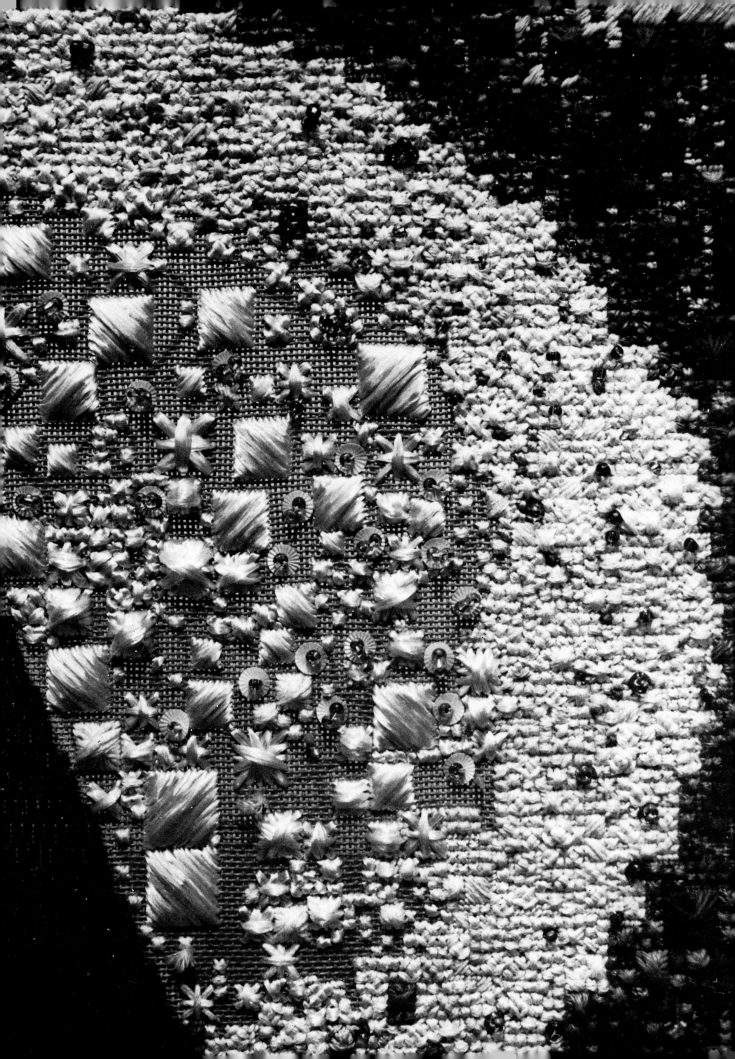

Assorted yarns suitable for working on canvas. Some of these yarns, such as the Salisbury cord, or the shiny lurex strip seen on the reel and the various strings, are only suitable as materials for couching down on canvas.

if they are strong and not too hairy. It is generally possible to divide the four-ply wools, if a thinner thread is required, but the twist must be put back into the thread after it has been divided.

If knitting wools are used, remember that they are a fashion product and colours are, therefore, liable to go off the market suddenly, if the manufacturers decide to discontinue a particular shade. If, therefore, you intend to use knitting wool to work a large area of background, for instance, it is advisable to purchase the full amount needed right at the start. Embroidery wools, on the other hand, are more reliable in this respect, and it is nearly always possible to repeat any shade of a colour year after year without any problems of matching-up. There is no actual difference in the quality of the two types of wool, and it is often very useful to keep a close eye on the knitting wool counter of the large shops for any unusual shade of wool or interesting textures.

Estimating yarn amounts

It is somewhat difficult to give exact estimates of the quantity of yarn required for working a given area on the various different meshes of canvas which might be used, but an approximate amount for working one square inch of tent stitch on 16 mesh single canvas would be 2 yards of crewel wool or a two-ply

Shetland knitting wool; for working the same area of tent stitch on a 24 mesh single canvas approximately $2\frac{3}{4}$ yards of silk or two-ply wool would be required; and for covering the same area when working with tent stitch on a very coarse mesh double canvas of say, 10/20 threads to the inch, and using a four-ply tapestry wool about $1\frac{1}{2}$ yards would be needed.

These are only very approximate quantities, as so much depends upon the individual person's method of working and the amount of wastage that is incurred. A better estimate may be achieved by working a square inch of the stitch to be used on a spare piece of canvas and then calculating the amounts needed to cover given areas in this stitch. But however the calculation is made, it will not be easy to arrive at more than a very rough estimate of the amounts of yarn required. To be sure that enough material is available, one should always estimate on the generous side.

Silk

Silk is best used for highlighting a design which is being worked mainly in wool or for working the background for such articles as evening bags, mirror surrounds, jewel boxes and other small things. A design carried out entirely in silk tends to be insipid in appearance and to lack character.

The best silk for canvas work is twisted embroidery silk. This silk is not stranded, and is easy to use. It is also possible to use a brand of silk, Filo Floss, but this is inclined to catch on everything and is, as a result, somewhat difficult to work with. Pure machine silk, which is sold on paper spools, is produced in two thicknesses. The thicker of the two can be used quite successfully on 16 mesh canvas if it is used double, but the colours available are more restricted than are those available in the finer thread. For working on 16 mesh canvas at least four threads of the finer silk has to be used at one time in the needle in order to cover the canvas properly.

Cotton, linen and synthetic threads

Anchor stranded cottons, DMC perle or other cotton pearl, coton-a-broder and many other types of cotton, linen, rayon and other synthetic yarns can also be used for canvas work, but, if the choice lies between using pure silk or cotton, either for highlights or for backgrounds, I should always prefer to use silk, as it has a lustre that no cotton yarn can rival: cotton worked over a large area can appear very heavy and solid, without the slightest trace of that brightness which silk can give. Rayon is not the easiest of materials to work with, as the thread has an unpleasant tendency to twist whilst being worked, and the worker has to spend time after every few stitches untwisting it before proceeding further.

Special yarns and unusual materials

For articles other than furniture coverings the choice of suitable yarns for working on canvas is very great and it is limited solely by the nature of the article. Some small objects, such as book-bindings, purses or dress ornaments, may require a much finer yarn than very large wall-hangings, but there is such a tremendous range of materials to choose from today that there should be no difficulty in finding something suitable for every purpose. In addition to the yarns already mentioned, others which can be used are lurex threads, Twilley's Goldfingering, made in many luscious colours, and the new Candlelite polyester and nylon yarns, made by Emu. These, together with carpet thrums, raffene, certain weaving yarns and various types of string make up a wide selection. Those kinds of string or unusual yarns that cannot be threaded through the holes in the canvas can still be used, if desired, by couching them down on the surface. Such things as gold and silver thread and various types of decorative leather, as well as beads and sequins can also be attached to the surface of the canvas. Even 'found objects' (objets trouvés) of all kinds, like shells picked up on the beach or interesting pieces of stone or tree-bark and attractive pieces of metal or glass, may also be used in this way. Care must be taken, however, to ensure that the applied objects are very securely attached and in some cases a touch of glue may be needed.

Needles

The needles used for working on canvas are both large-eyed and blunt-pointed; they are called tapestry needles and are obtainable in many sizes from 13 to 26, the larger needles having the smaller numbers. For a particular piece of work, the most suitable needle will have an eye large enough to allow the chosen yarn to be threaded easily, but not so large that the needle is constantly becoming unthreaded. The eye of the needle must also pass smoothly through the holes in the canvas without displacing at all the threads of the canvas. A good average size of needle for this work is 18 or 20, 18 being best for 16 mesh and 20 for 18 mesh canvas. A 14 or 16 needle can prove useful for working with very coarse wools, such as carpet thrums, on a 12 or 14 mesh canvas, and a 26 needle should be a suitable size to use when working with fine wool or with one or two strands of silk on a fine canvas.

Two simple home-made rectangular frames, showing two methods of joining the corners.

Frames

Canvas work is generally done on an embroidery frame, but small articles can, if necessary, be worked in the hand. The advantages of working on a frame are that it helps to keep the canvas taut making it easier to work and, most important point of all, limits the danger that the finished piece of embroidery may be pulled out of shape. If the canvas is held in the hand for working, the stitches, especially tent stitch, tend to pull the work out of the square, and a large piece of work requires quite an amount of skill and a great deal of energy to restore it to its original shape.

There are several different types of frame to choose from. The very simplest one, and one which can easily be made at home, is a rectangular frame made from $2\frac{1}{2}$ inch by $1\frac{3}{4}$ inch battens, nailed together at each corner. Such a frame must be large enough to take the whole extent of the canvas to be worked, which cannot be rolled up as on other types of frame, but is fixed to the edges of the frame all round with $\frac{3}{8}$ inch tacks or stapling. This frame is, therefore, only suitable for pieces of work which are not very large.

A second type of frame, and one which I prefer for canvas work,

A very small flat-bar frame with a piece of work mounted.

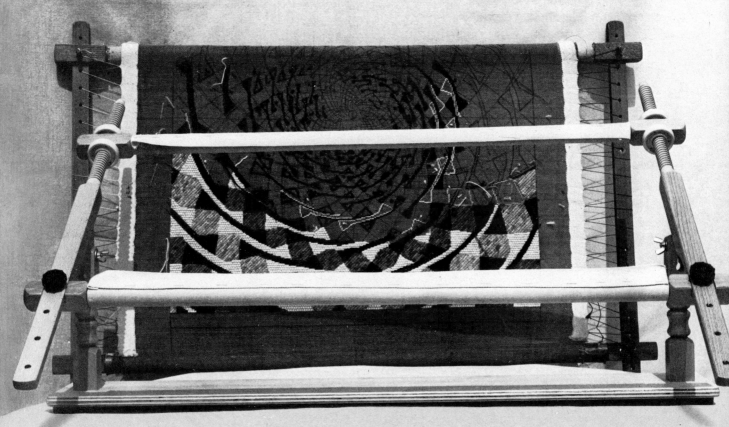

is the flat-bar type. It consists of two rollers, one for the top edge of the frame and one for the bottom, and two flat wooden side pieces with holes drilled in them at intervals to take split pins (cotter pins) or wooden pegs. The ends of these side pieces are put through large slots at the ends of the rollers and are held in position by the split pins or wooden pegs. This frame can also be made quite easily at home: a wooden broom handle can be cut to the required size and used for the rollers and split pins can be obtained from cycle or car supply shops.

In order to fix the canvas to such a frame, it is necessary to have a piece of strong, 2 inch wide tape or webbing stretched along the full length of both rollers and tacked down with tin tacks at one inch intervals. It is advisable not to use dome-headed nails for this, as they will mark the canvas, if it has to be rolled up. The centre line should be marked in permanently on the two tapes attached to the rollers.

A third type of embroidery frame, which can also be used for canvas work, is the screw-bar frame. This frame is similar to the flat-bar type, but the side pieces which fit into the rollers at the top and bottom of the frame have a screw-thread at each end and are held in position by circular wooden rings, two of which screw on at each end of the side bars, one on either side of the rollers, and

Another flat-bar frame, showing the double line of holes with cotter pins in position, which are used to enable the size of the frame to be varied and the work to be put under tension. ◁

Two frames are seen here; the back one is a normal flat-bar type with a piece of work mounted; the front one is a sturdy table frame which has features of both screw-bar and flat-bar types. ◁▽

A well-made floor model with a detachable screw-bar frame. The whole assemblage can easily be dismounted for storing. ▽

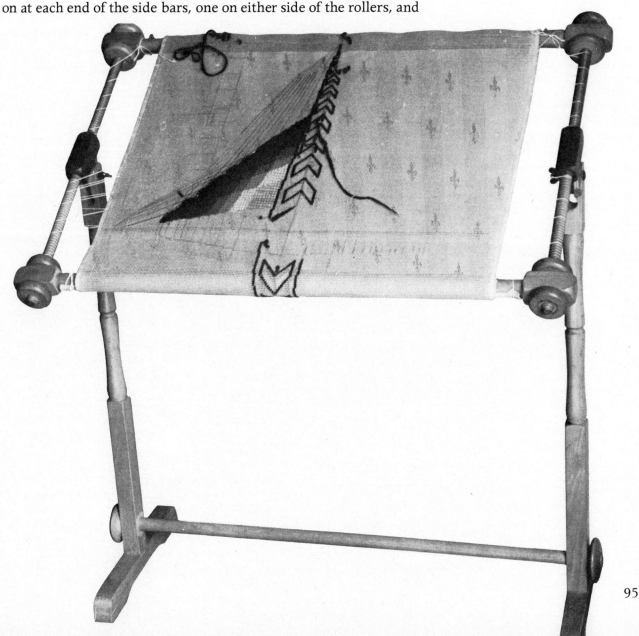

are tightened up to hold the frame rigid. One disadvantage of this frame is, however, that, when the canvas is pulled absolutely taut, as it should be for the best results, the frame is inclined to twist and refuse to lie flat. A further disadvantage is that the canvas on the screw-bar frame cannot be rolled up to give such a small working area as can be achieved with the flat-bar type of frame. This occurs because the movement of the rollers is limited by the shortness of the screw-thread on the side bars.

Both the flat-bar and the screw-bar types of frame can be purchased from most shops dealing with embroidery requisites, and there are others of varying sizes, such as the small travelling frames, which are also quite suitable for canvas work. The circular ring frames known as tambour frames are, however, not at all suitable for this work, and, if the canvas to be worked is so small as to fit one of these circular frames, it is really better, in my opinion, to do the work in the hand and to dispense with a frame altogether.

When purchasing a frame, it is essential to state the length of the tape required. Frames are made with 24 inch, 27 inch and 36 inch tapes, which means that they will accommodate 24 inch, 27 inch or 36 inch widths of canvas.

6 Starting to work

Transferring designs to canvas

Your design has been finally decided upon and drawn out on paper. Now outline it in black, using either a felt-tipped pen or a brush and water-colour paint. The vertical and horizontal centre lines are drawn in pencil right across the design and the intersection of these centre lines should be marked in clearly to give a small cross in the centre of the design. The four points where the centre lines meet the outside edges of the design should also be marked in in black.

The piece of canvas on to which the design is to be traced should be two inches larger all round than the design and should also have its vertical and horizontal centre lines marked in pencil. To do this, fold the canvas over squarely one way and mark where the centre fold comes. Open the canvas again and hold a pencil on the centre fold so that it is directly between two threads. Draw the pencil down between the threads to make an accurate straight line right

This picture shows the design pinned in position under the canvas, with the centre lines marked in and the tracing just started with black paint.

across the centre of the canvas. Repeat the same process at right angles through the centre point.

Place the design on a drawing-board, and pin the canvas in position over it with drawing pins or thumb tacks, so that the centre lines on the canvas exactly match those of the design. This is best done by first placing a drawing pin directly in the centre of the work, using the black cross which indicates the exact centre of the design. Spread the canvas out from the centre and pin it down so that the points where the centre lines meet the outer edges of the canvas match these same points on the design. It may be necessary to pull the canvas to get it into the correct position before finally pinning it down all round.

The outline of the design should now be clearly visible through the canvas, and tracing can begin. If, however, there is difficulty in seeing the design through the canvas, it may be because it has been drawn on thin paper, such as greaseproof or tracing paper, and this can often be remedied by placing a piece of plain white paper underneath the original drawing. In certain lights it is helpful to shade with the hand that part of the design being traced, in order to prevent a heavy shadow of the canvas mesh from obscuring the line of the design.

Trace the design using a number 5 sable brush and black water-colour paint, mixed on the dry side. A felt-tipped pen can be used for tracing, but the line made by such a pen can rub off and mark light-coloured silk or wool, unless the pen is waterproof.

If preferred, the design can be traced on to the canvas after it has been attached to the frame. In this case the paper design is pinned in position underneath the canvas, and the frame may be moved around to get it into a position where the lines of the design are clearly visible for tracing.

Fixing the canvas on to the frame

Before attaching the canvas to the frame, four threads on the edge should be turned under and the pencilled centre line matched exactly to the centre line on one of the tapes or strips of webbing already fixed to the rollers of the frame. Starting from the centre point and pulling both canvas and webbing taut, oversew the two edges with strong sewing cotton, working outwards from the centre, first to one edge of the canvas and then to the other and fastening off the thread securely at both ends. Attach the opposite edge of the piece of canvas to the other roller in the same manner.

The canvas can now be rolled up to a convenient size and the side struts put into position through the slots at each end of the rollers and fixed by means of the split pins. Fix one roller first and then stretch the canvas to its fullest extent before fixing the other roller in position. When it is ready for working, the canvas should be as tight as a drum, and to achieve this, sew a piece of webbing securely down each side of the canvas and lace it to the side struts by means of a packing needle and fine strong twine, which should pass over the side struts at intervals of about one inch. Fasten the twine off securely. The pieces of webbing thus used must only be as long as the sides of the canvas exposed for working on the surface of the frame and must not be wound around the rollers, as this would cause a tightening-up of the edges of the

Here we see the method of lacing the edges of the canvas to the side bar of a flat-bar frame. △

A method of tying the edge of the canvas to the side bar of a screw-bar frame with individual ties. ▽

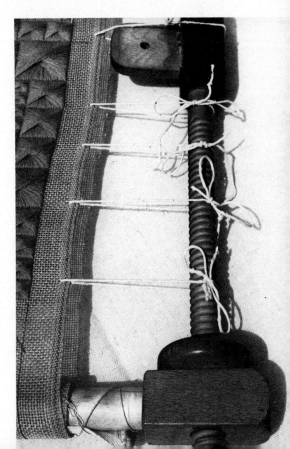

100

canvas, whilst the centre remained slack. When it is necessary to move the canvas by winding it off one roller and onto the other, the webbing must be removed from the edges and then re-attached, when the new area of canvas has been exposed.

When one is actually working a piece of canvas embroidery on a frame, it is essential that the frame is correctly positioned. The screw-bar type of frame can be bought with its own proper floor stand, and the work can be fixed in a comfortable position for the worker, so that she can have her hands completely free to manipulate needle and thread. Other types of frame can be placed so that they are supported between the worker and the edge of the table, or, better still, between the edges of two tables or two trestles placed near to one another. The idea is to leave both hands of the worker quite free for the actual work of embroidery: one hand should be kept above the canvas stretched on the frame and the other beneath it, thus enabling the needle to be passed quickly up and down through the holes in the canvas and also ensuring a good, even finish to the work.

Method of working

To begin canvas embroidery take a strand of yarn measuring about twenty-four inches in length. Anything longer than this is too long, because the continual movement of the yarn, as it passes up and down through the canvas causes it to fray and wear very thin. It is good practice, before using a length of wool, to pull it between the first finger and thumb nail of one hand in order to remove all surplus fluff, which may otherwise clog the holes in the canvas, thus helping to weaken the thread and causing it to break.

Make a knot at the end of the thread, and take the needle down through the canvas to the underside a short distance away from the point where the work is to start, leaving the knot on the surface. When that particular length of yarn is finished, the end of the thread should be brought up to the surface of the canvas again a short distance away from the last stitch worked. Thus the work is continued, with the knots and the ends of the threads left upon the surface of the canvas until the short lengths of yarn, which have been left beneath the surface, have been caught in and covered by subsequent stitches; the knots and loose ends of the thread may then be cut off. This way of working, which keeps all

An altar frontal partly-worked. This piece is being worked differently from the usual practice of beginning with the area of design and not with the background. The reason for this change of method is that the small central design motif is to be worked with padded gold leather and large circular jewels, and this will prevent the possibility of rolling up this central area of the canvas on to the frame. The method of working to be adopted, therefore, in this case is to complete working the background areas at each end of this long panel first, so that they can be rolled on to the frame and will allow the central section to be held rigid whilst the final working is put in.

101

the knots and loose ends of yarn upon the surface of the work, leaves the back completely free of obstruction and facilitates the process of the embroidering.

Sometimes the yarn may break during working. This can happen if the ply of the wool becomes untwisted, and it is, therefore, a good idea to try to prevent this from happening by occasionally giving a half twist to the needle in the direction in which the ply had been originally twisted, or one can simply let the needle hang down for a moment, so that it will automatically twist the thread back to normal. If more than one thread is being used in the needle, it requires care to see that the threads do not become twisted around one another during the working, as this can give an uneven finish to the work.

When starting a new piece of canvas work, the embroiderer is advised to begin by working a part of the design and not to work the background first. There is always a tendency, when one is working on canvas, to encroach somewhat on to threads of the canvas surrounding the area being worked. If, therefore, areas of background are put in first, one can easily lose the true outline of a shape or reduce its full effect in the design. Even when one has begun correctly by working a part of the design first, it is still possible to lose the true outline of the chosen shape. This is especially likely when square stitches are being used to fill an area bounded by curves. The best way to proceed in this case is to work carefully in tent stitch the curved outline of the area about to be worked before the remainder of the shape is filled in. Tent stitch is the smallest stitch in canvas work and is ideal for working on curved lines and this method of working enables the embroiderer to keep closely to the lines of the design. It also prevents the awkward and unsightly stepped effect which is caused if square stitches are used alone to fill a shape which is bounded by curves.

When working an area on canvas in which the colours are shaded from dark to light, it is also important to remember the effect of the possible encroachment of one shade upon another. In this case the worker should first decide if the effect required is to be on the darker side or on the lighter side. If a lighter effect is desired, then work should begin with the silk highlight and the paler shades, but, if a darker effect is sought, then the darker areas should be worked first.

However carefully one works, sometimes a stitch is sure to be put in in the wrong place, but do not allow this to disturb you unduly. It may be possible to correct a wrong stitch by working another stitch over it, but generally this can only be done successfully when wool is used to make the correction. If silk is being used, it may fail to cover the mistake completely. If this type of correction proves impossible to work, never hesitate to unpick a section of the work and start again.

Even if a design has been worked carefully and accurately, it sometimes becomes apparent to the worker that the effect being produced is not quite as was originally intended or that the colour scheme has developed elements which are disturbing. At this point, thought must be given to possible alterations. Do not despair, but realize that it is seldom possible to complete a piece of work exactly as it was planned. It is by a constant creative process during the working that a really successful result is achieved:

102

'Sea Spirit'. When careful thought has been given to the choice and size of stitches, and a well-considered colour scheme has been adopted, a few lines traced on to the canvas can be transformed into a very bold, striking and attractive panel. The method of first outlining the design shapes can be clearly seen. This panel may be seen in colour on page 61.

This shows the best method of working on canvas with one hand above and one below the surface of the work. A few threads of the canvas have been turned under and attached to the tape, and it demonstrates the method of starting work with a knot on the surface and finishing a length of yarn by bringing the end back up to the surface of the canvas. A screw-bar frame is being used on a table.

A detail of the 'Seashore' panel, shown on pages 2–3, showing felt and gold leather being applied. △

'Mexico'. This picture shows the usual method of working on canvas with all the principal lines of the design first outlined in tent stitch before the various square stitches are worked. This method preserves the good lines of the original drawing and prevents ugly 'stepped' effects. ◁

A detail of a panel which shows how jewels may be stitched on to gold leather so that they are fully integrated into it. The jewels were inserted into holes cut in the leather and stitched down. Long stitches of silk were then radiated from the edge of the jewels on to the leather, and gold-fingering was woven over and under these stitches. ▷

This shows how the smooth surface of the gold leather, outlined with gold thread, forms a strong contrast to the four roundels of gold leather on the dark brown ground, which are covered with a surface decoration of thin gold thread. This decorative covering of thread has been applied by putting a circle of it in the middle of the circular shape and button-holing round it. ◁

In this small, unfinished panel, pieces of Victorian jet beadwork have been carefully applied to the canvas. This not only helps to preserve them, but, by associating them with modern jewels and stitchery, it is possible to create a pleasing design. ◁

An exercise to show ways of attaching various 'found objects' to the canvas. △

Cutting holes in the canvas. A piece of fabric has been placed behind the canvas to show the intricate pattern of holes which have been cut out of the canvas. One hole at a time was cut and carefully oversewn. ◁

An exercise which shows how a papier mâché ball can be incorporated in a panel by cutting a hole in the canvas and suspending the ball in the opening by means of threads passed through it. △

the basic design and colour scheme simply give a foundation upon which you will build, sometimes altering original ideas, sometimes removing certain elements altogether and sometimes adding completely new ones. When considering colour and texture, it is always helpful from time to time during the working of a piece of canvas embroidery to place it at a distance and to look at it from different angles in order to observe and then correct any items in the design which no longer seem completely satisfying. It is a very good plan to leave a partly worked piece of embroidery in a permanent position in a room for several days, so that it can be carefully observed in differing lights, and ideas for further development can be experimented with by, for instance, attaching to it other pieces of material temporarily, either to obscure something which seems out of place, or to suggest additional elements that may be used to improve the design.

Shapes in card, made from colour slide mounts, have been used as a base for working over with long stitches. ▽

7 What to make

Canvas embroidery is very suitable for making delightful, small articles to have around the home and for attractive dress accessories. Such things as jewellery boxes, pincushions, spectacle- and comb cases, day and evening bags, purses, collars, belts, etc. are not only pleasing things to look at but they are also delightful to work. Being small, they are worked in the hand without a frame and can, therefore, be picked up at any moment and are usually completed in a very short time, before the initial enthusiasm can wear off. They form wonderful, little gifts which are much appreciated on occasions such as birthdays and Christmas. There is just one reservation, which I personally would make in regard to this last idea; I would only send such gifts to someone whom I knew would fully appreciate the time and thought which had gone into the making of them.

Boxes

What could be more individual, than to make and embroider a circular or rectangular box to hold special, favourite pieces of

This circular jewel box was made of cardboard and covered with canvas embroidery. ◁

A tin box covered with canvas work on the top and with silk on the sides. Gold gimp has been used for finishing. ▽

A small box being made out of cardboard. ▷

Diagram for a square box. ▽

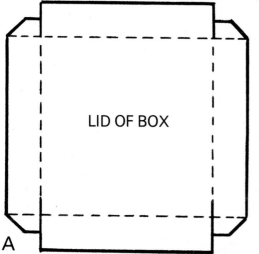

LID OF BOX

A

BASE OF BOX

B

PATTERN FOR
FABRIC COVERING
FOR BASE

C

jewellery and small dress accessories? Beautifully worked, and possibly decorated themselves with jewels, embroidered boxes can be made worthy to adorn the dressing-tables of even the most fastidious.

Begin by taking a paper pattern of an existing box and work a cover for it. Pin the pattern to the canvas and mark round it with a felt-tipped pen. It is then ready for working. A very simple design can be drawn directly on to the canvas, or, if preferred, some beads, a jewel or a polished stone can be attached securely to the canvas to form a centre of interest, and suitable stitches worked in an attractive colour-scheme around it.

If, however, a box of a particular size or shape is required, this can be made from cardboard. The diagrams on page 110 show how to make a square box, but the instructions can be adapted for making a rectangular box of any size. Cut out the box base and the lid and assemble them by gluing. Cover both box and lid with either paper or a thin material, such as butter muslin, to strengthen them. Place the worked canvas for the box lid face downwards on a board, and lightly glue the lid upon it, centring it. Turn up the embroidered sides against the sides of the lid. Fold and cut corners as shown in the lid diagram. Cut the surplus canvas away, so that there is finally a border of half an inch of unworked canvas left all round to be turned under and glued down. Where the areas of worked canvas on each side of the lid meet at the corners, turn the narrow border of unworked canvas under and sew the edges of the worked part together. Cover the sides and outer bottom of the box either with a piece of material or with another piece of worked canvas. If canvas is used, it should, as before, have a narrow, unworked border which may be turned under at top and bottom before the whole is glued to the sides of the box. Attach the lid to the back of the box either by over-sewing or by gluing on hinges made of narrow tape.

The interior of the box is finished off by cutting a piece of card to fit the inside base. Pad it slightly with thin cotton wool or a piece of felt, covered with lining silk. Glue it carefully upon the base inside. Finally, cut a collar of thin card, to the total width of the four sides and to the same depth as the box is on the outside. Fold and crease the strip so that it fits inside the box. Pad the collar piece slightly and cover it with lining silk. Fit and glue the collar in position. The fact that the depth of the collar of card is the same as the depth of the box outside causes its top edge to be raised slightly above the sides of the box, when it is glued inside. This enables the lid to fit snugly upon the box, when it is closed. Finally, line the lid in a similar way, but without the collar of card. Glue a piece of felt or baize on the underside of the box to finish.

Paper weights

Large pebbles, gathered from the garden or the beach, can be covered with canvas embroidery to make lovely paper weights.

Choose a large, round pebble about two inches (five cm.) across. Place it on a piece of paper and, with a pencil held vertically pressing against the side of the stone, draw a line all round it. This will give a template to mark on the canvas and indicate the size and shape to work the embroidery.

Attractive paper weights can be made by covering large pebbles with canvas work and leather.

111

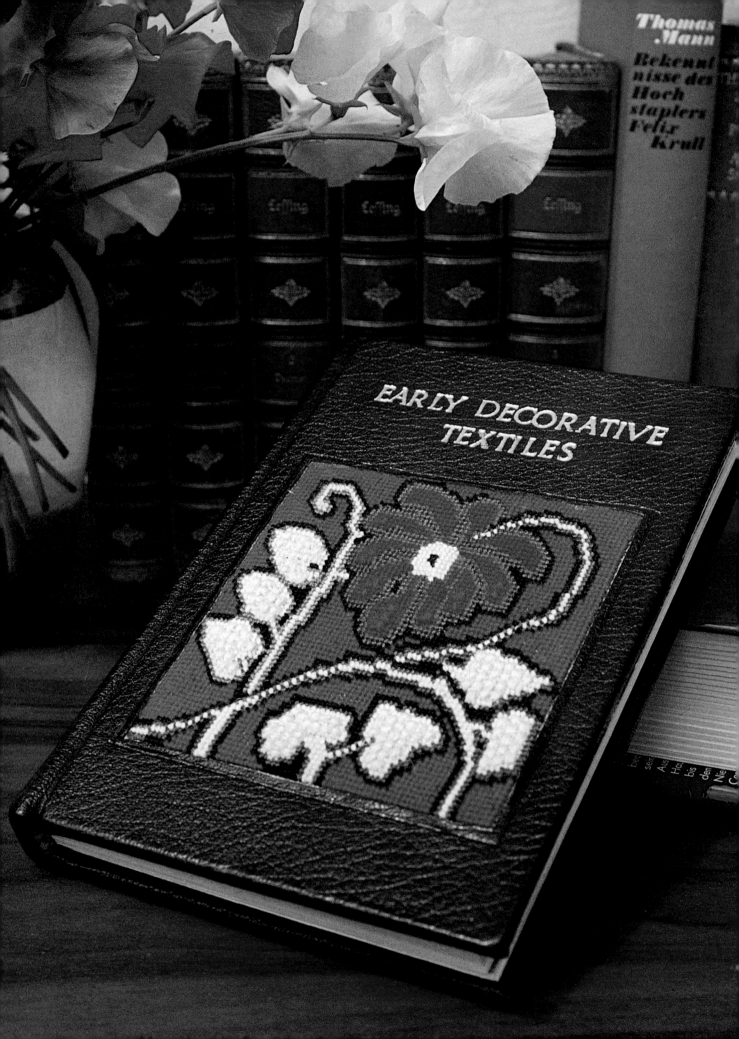

A small panel of canvas embroidery has been set into the leather binding for a special book. ◁

Designs to work for door finger-plates. △▷

Two perspex door finger-plates with canvas work insets. ▷▷

To mount the finished embroidery, cut a piece of cardboard to the size of the template and stick it to the under-side of the pebble with strong adhesive such as Uhu to form a nice flat base. Cut away all surplus canvas around the embroidered area, leaving a narrow border to hold the work when it is glued to the stone. It may be necessary to cut small snippets out of this unworked border to enable the canvas to be shaped to the curves of the pebble. Pack around the undersides of the pebble with twists of paper, which should also be stuck in position with strong adhesive. Cover the sides of the paper weight with a circlet of thin card, by cutting out a piece just deep enough to fit between the edges of the embroidered surface and the base of the weight and long enough to extend all round. Glue it to the sides of the pebble. Cover the circlet with a strip of worked canvas or a piece of felt or fabric. Glue this in position, and join the edges of the three surfaces together by over-sewing round the top and bottom seams. Cut a piece of thin leather or felt to fit the bottom. If preferred, a box shape just large enough to take the pebble can be made from cardboard, the pebble placed inside it and held firmly in position by small wads of paper. Cover the sides of the box and the top of the stone with canvas embroidery.

Alternatively, glass paper weights can be bought, which have a recess at the base for taking a small piece of embroidery.

Finger plates for doors

Finger plates incorporating small pieces of embroidery worked on fine mesh canvas (20 threads to one inch) can look very attractive,

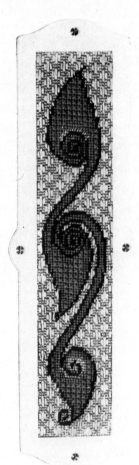

113

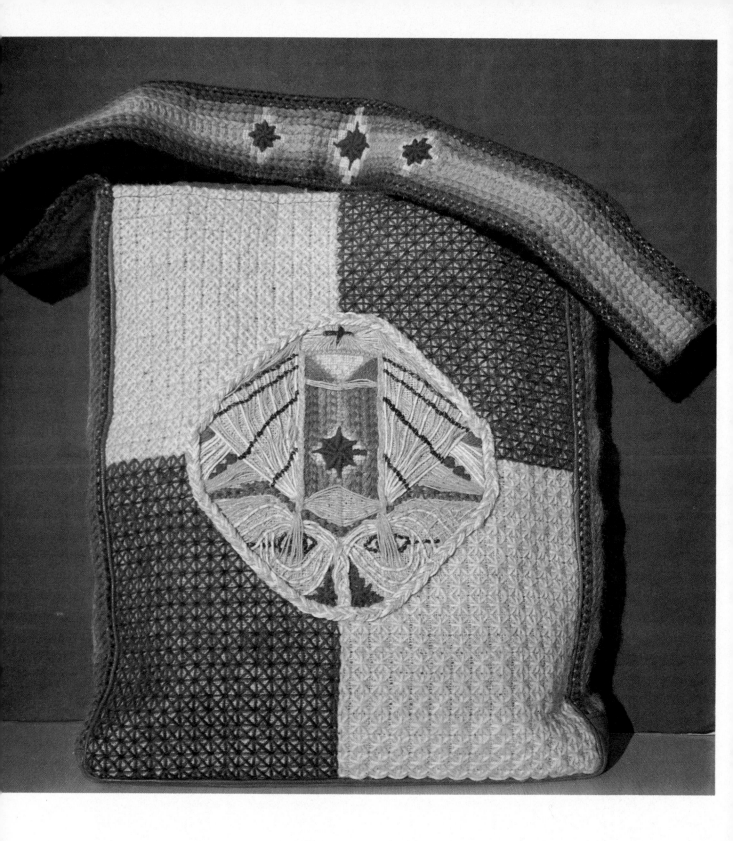

A capacious shoulder bag.
Canvas threads, brought
through to the front of the work
and couched down, make an
unusual and interesting bag. △
114

A charming little cushion for the
patio, worked entirely in cross
stitch with large and small
smyrna stitches superimposed at
random. ▷

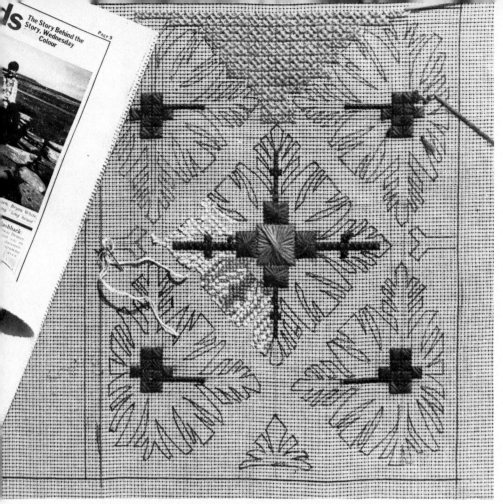

A partly-worked loose cover for a magazine, on double-thread canvas. The diagrams below show how the design was developed by folding a square of paper and cutting it. The paper was opened out, and the resulting shape placed under tracing paper and traced. The centre lines were marked in. The centre of the canvas was also marked and was placed over the tracing paper. The design was traced through on to the canvas. It is necessary to move the canvas around in order to trace on the motif at each corner. Adapt the design by reducing the area at the sides. ◁

This evening bag is worked entirely in metallized thread, with gold leather and jewels applied. The background is worked in smyrna stitch, surrounded by tent stitch. ▷

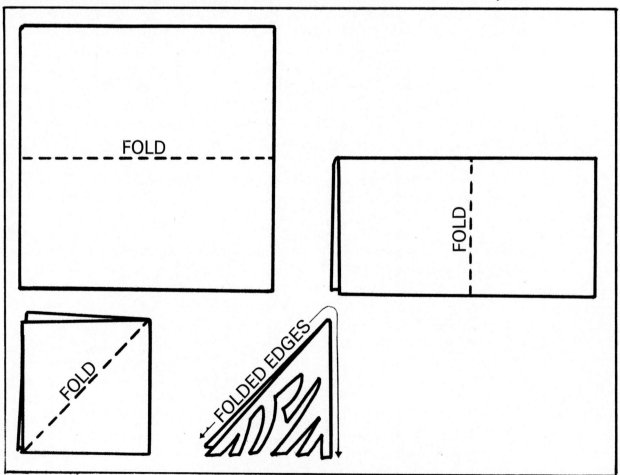

particularly if the design is worked in wool and the background in silk. The colouring should not be too dominant and should be planned to be acceptable in any room. Only flat stitches can be used in the working. Both the fingerplates illustrated consist of a perspex (plexiglas) base, out of which a central recess has been cut to take a piece of canvas work, and a perspex cover which has been fixed down exactly upon the base with strong adhesive. The whole finger plate is fixed to the door with screws.

Evening bags

A suitable metal frame on which to mount the finished canvas work should be obtained before starting to work out the shape and the design for the bag. There are some quite inexpensive frames obtainable, but it pays to buy the best that one can afford, as the nature of the frame and of the handle makes all the difference to the finished article.

The illustrations on pages 117 and 118 show a selection of attractive evening bags. They have been worked with the backgrounds either in pure silk, or in gold or silver metallized threads, and in neutral shades which will go well with a variety of dress colours. Evening bags can have a more luxurious look than every-

A black leather handbag of the flap-over type. A small rectangle of canvas work has been skilfully mounted in leather to make an outstanding and attractive bag. △

A small purse worked in diagonal and tent stitches on a mosaic stitch background. The design and colouring were taken from the hearts-ease flower. ▽

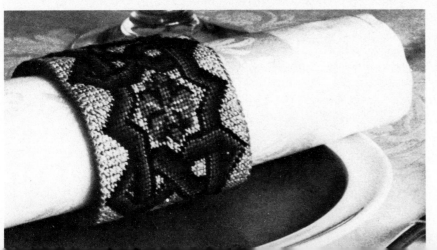

The design for this table-napkin ring was adapted from an Elizabethan cushion. It is worked in tent stitch on a silk background of mosaic stitch. ◁

Turquoise, brown and silver collar. An unusual and strikingly original collar. The outer edges are oversewn with metallized thread, as are the edges of the cut-away areas. Large, square wooden beads are stitched in position, and turquoise-coloured diamond shapes in satin stitch are worked beside them. A single row of tent stitch, also in turquoise, outlines the silver edges of the collar. The background, which is worked in cross stitch in mahogany-brown and black, has four large rectangular shapes cut out of it, and two rows of tiny wooden beads have been strung across the openings. ◁

Brightly-coloured handbag in a geometric design. ▷

The background of this evening bag is worked entirely in cushion stitch, in twisted embroidery silk. Gold leather and couched gold threads are used, with jewels. ◁

Everyday handbag. What could be nicer than to work this handbag to match a scarf? ▷

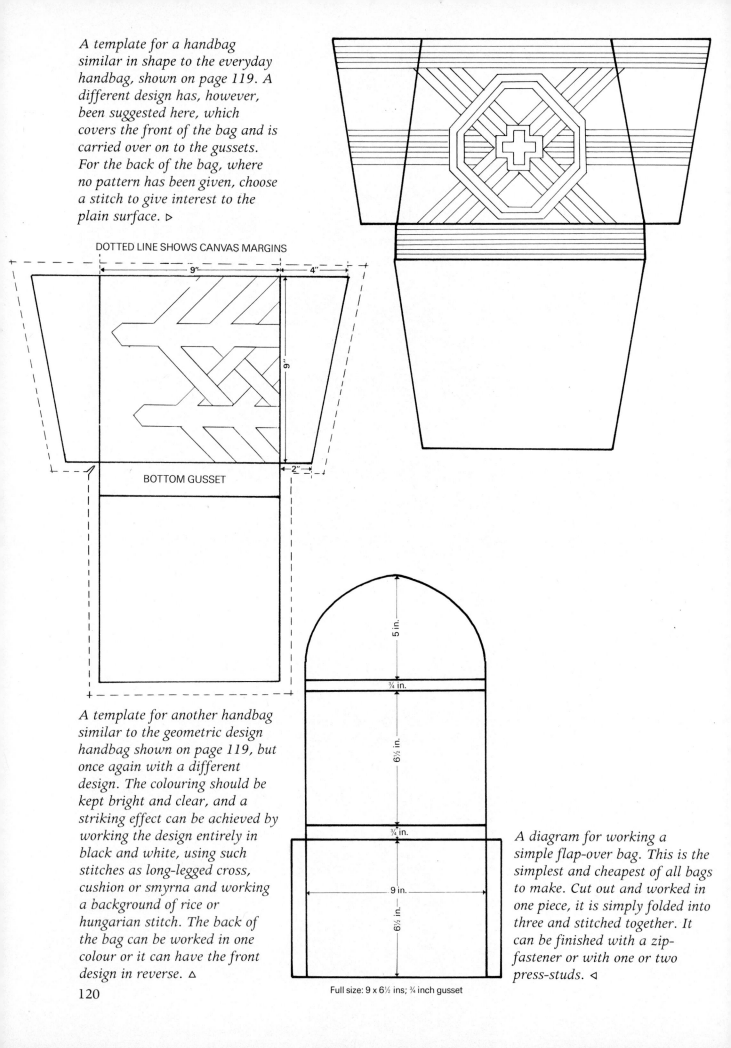

A template for a handbag similar in shape to the everyday handbag, shown on page 119. A different design has, however, been suggested here, which covers the front of the bag and is carried over on to the gussets. For the back of the bag, where no pattern has been given, choose a stitch to give interest to the plain surface. ▷

DOTTED LINE SHOWS CANVAS MARGINS

9"　　4"

9"

BOTTOM GUSSET

2"

A template for another handbag similar to the geometric design handbag shown on page 119, but once again with a different design. The colouring should be kept bright and clear, and a striking effect can be achieved by working the design entirely in black and white, using such stitches as long-legged cross, cushion or smyrna and working a background of rice or hungarian stitch. The back of the bag can be worked in one colour or it can have the front design in reverse. △

120

5 in.

¾ in.

6½ in.

¾ in.

9 in.

6½ in.

Full size: 9 x 6½ ins; ¾ inch gusset

A diagram for working a simple flap-over bag. This is the simplest and cheapest of all bags to make. Cut out and worked in one piece, it is simply folded into three and stitched together. It can be finished with a zip-fastener or with one or two press-studs. ◁

page 123
A versatile bolero is something quite new for working in canvas.

This belt has a liberal display of topaz and amethyst jewels and gold leather. The background is worked in orange variegated stranded cotton. This gives a charming broken effect to the colouring, but care should be taken in using it, as there is little control of the colour. It should only be used if a really haphazard colour effect is required.

A small sea-horse was first attached to the canvas ground and surrounded with an irregular line of tent stitch in emerald green goldfingering. An emerald jewel was attached to the canvas within the curve of the sea-horse's tail, and the whole was completed by working a pattern of irregular lines in black wool and green goldfingering in tent stitch upon a background of rice stitch, worked in gold metallic thread. Small copper beads form a border all round the pendant and some other beads of various sizes are suspended from the lower edge of the pendant. The backing is a piece of tin covered with gold leather. It measures 2¾ inches by 2¼ inches.

Blue and green silk and silver thread have been used with pearls to make this pendant. Lines in tent stitch radiate from two dark curved areas of mosaic stitch, which support a central panel, worked in smyrna stitch, french knots and straight stitch, upon which the pearls are placed. The dimensions are 3 inches by 2¼ inches.

day handbags and the canvas work can be embellished with beads and jewels.

These two evening bags were professionally made up. This, of course, adds to the cost of making, but, unless you are confident of being able to carry out this work, it is worth having it done.

Everyday handbags

Handbags for everyday use will naturally be somewhat less glamorous than evening bags, but they can still be gay and attractive. Furthermore, a handbag is the kind of article which can be something completely individual, and this in itself can make the idea of working one in canvas embroidery attractive. By using the type of handbag frame on which the worked canvas is folded over a rod on each side, and is easily attached and detached, it is possible to work and have ready for use several different embroidered covers – a handbag for every occasion and for every colour scheme.

These bags are quite simple to make up. Two of the diagrams (opposite) show clearly how to cut out the sides and gusset. The depth of the bag should be approximately the same as the width of the metal frame. The lining and interlining are cut to the same size as the bag. In order to allow the bag to stand properly, cut a piece of medium to thick card to fit the bottom gusset and either stitch it in with herringbone stitching, or glue it in position to the interlining. Take the raw edge of the canvas at the top of the work over the rods and stitch it to make a small open-ended hem to hold the rods. Place the lining inside and slip-stitch all round. The needlework is held entirely by the two rods, which can be unscrewed and removed at any time to allow another piece of work to be attached.

Flap-over type of bag

This type of bag is the easiest of all bags to make, as the back, front and flap-over panels and the gussets can all be worked in one piece, lower diagram, opposite. The design should be mainly on the flap, with a somewhat smaller motif on the back. The gusset can be worked plain or in a pattern. A card cut to fit the bottom gusset helps to keep the base firm. The lining and interlining are also cut to the same measurements.

A handle can be worked on canvas to fit the bag and this should be approximately one inch (2·5 cm.) wide and to any length required. Turn the edges of the canvas back and oversew closely with the background wool, to prevent the canvas from fraying. Stitch the handle firmly to the top of the bag directly underneath the gusset allowance, where the back section and the front flap meet. A zip-fastener can also be sewn in, if needed.

The bag illustrated on page 117 has a panel of canvas work set in leather, but any suitable strong fabric can be used instead of leather. The exact size of the needlework panel was marked on to the leather, and the aperture for the panel then cut from the centre outwards to each corner, the spare material being turned under to the back of the work and either stuck or tacked down. This provided a mount, which was then placed over the embroidered panel and stitched firmly all round.

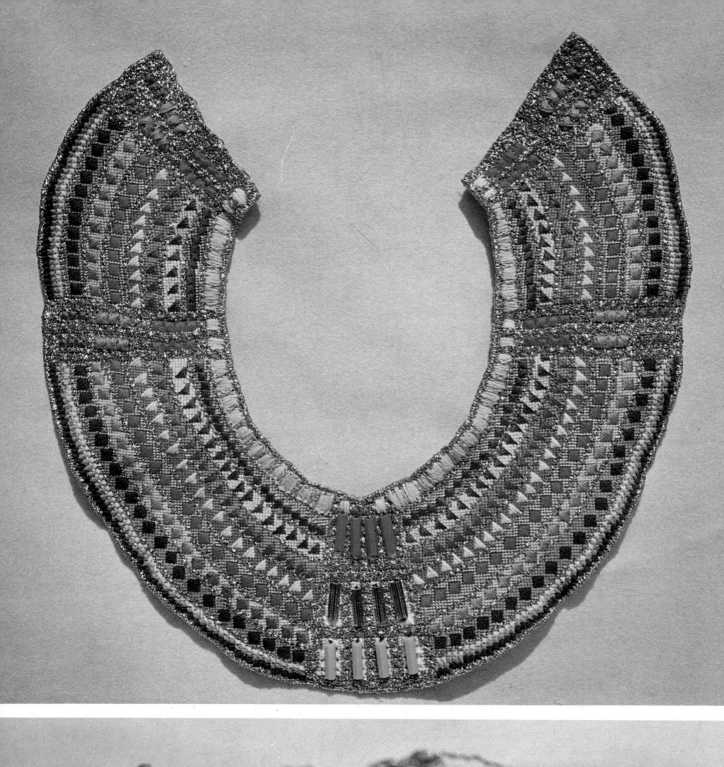

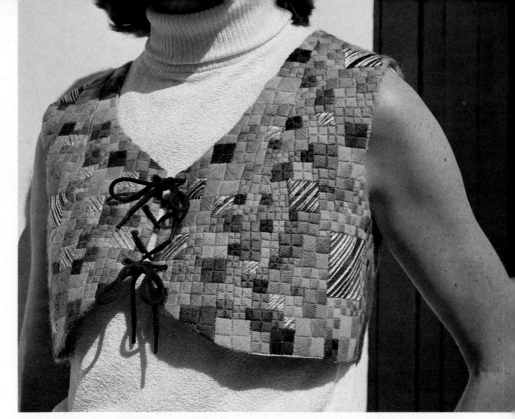

A spectacular collar for a very special occasion. The creation of this collar was inspired by the famous collars of the Pharaohs, but, whereas their collars were made of beads, this one has been worked with silk, cotton, wool and metal thread in many stitches upon canvas and has only a few long bugle beads attached to the centre-front. The fastening for this collar is at the back. ◁

Mingled beads and stitches make a neck band which is a pretty ornament too. ◁ ▽

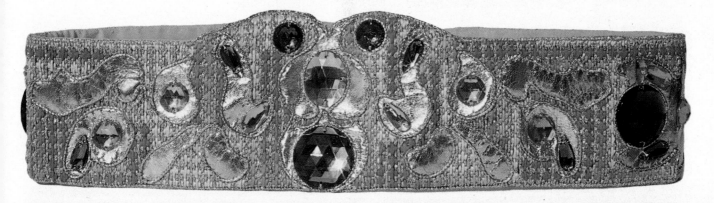

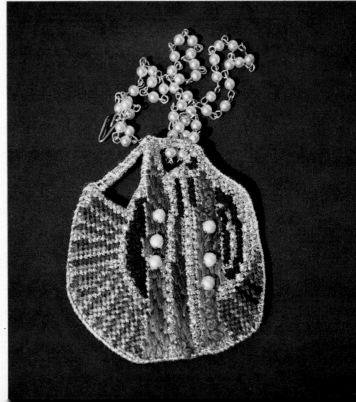

Little pincushions make lovely small presents, especially when the colouring is gay.

This book-mark, for a special occasion gift, is worked in silk, wool and metallized thread on fine canvas (24 threads to the inch). It is worked in tent stitch in shades of gold. ◁

The idea for these attractive little book-marks was derived from the now rare ornamental markers of the early seventeenth century. △

A group of decorative and varied spectacle-cases.

This lapel is worked on 16 mesh canvas so that it is pliable enough for the purpose. It is worked in tent stitch in emerald green coton a broder with smyrna stitch in goldfingering, on a white background of rice stitch.

125

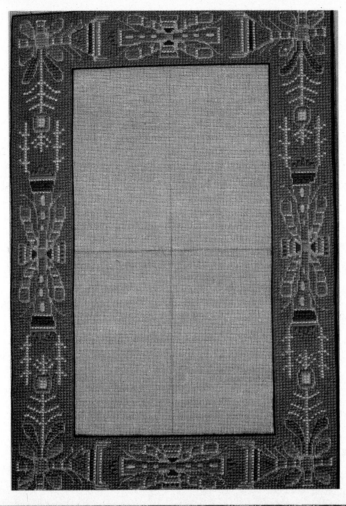

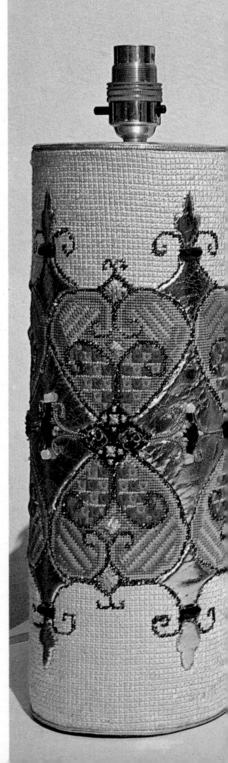

A finished canvas for a mirror surround before mounting. The central area of canvas will be removed and the worked surround mounted on hardboard.◁

A mirror surround which has been mounted on bevelled glass and framed. A simple leaf design has been treated here in a stylized way, which is very suitable for such a piece of work.

A group of four table lamps
after making up. ▽

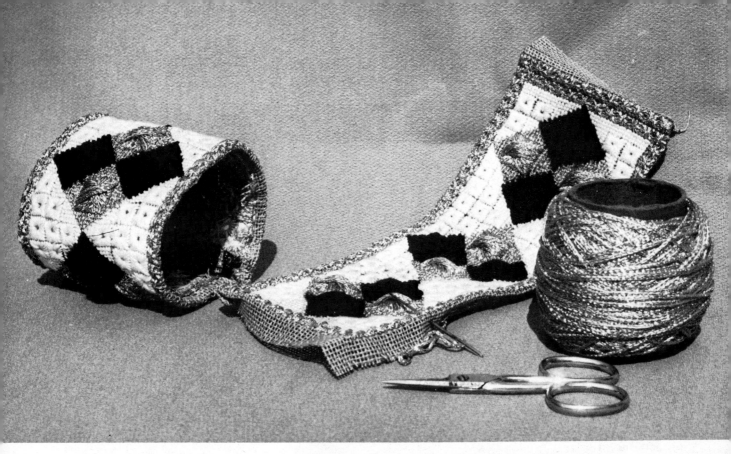

These cuffs are worked in black
wool, white cotton and
goldfingering. The canvas is
shown being turned under and
stitched in position with a
back stitch. The cuffs are
afterwards lined with silk or
other suitable fabric. △

Small sections of worked canvas
are linked together by thonging
to form a most attractive belt.
Each section is finished with an
edging in the form of a thin cord
of silk and metal thread.

This belt has the edges all
overcast with the same coloured
wool as that used for working.
It is a shaped belt, with the
extra width in the centre section
of the belt worked in rice stitch.

128

A partly-worked belt, showing how button-hole edging can be used in place of the usual overcasting. Smyrna and tent stitches have been used.

A harlequin belt with edges oversewn and fastened with suede thonging. The dark green of the background sets off well the gay colouring of the diamond pattern.

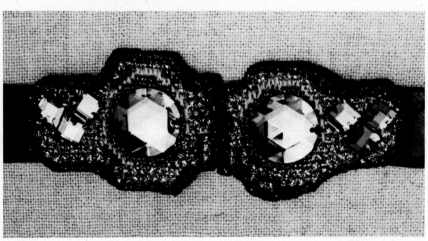

A clasp for a belt on an evening gown. Two large blue jewels and six smaller square ones were stitched firmly on to the canvas ground. The canvas edges were turned under and oversewn with emerald-coloured metallized thread. Smyrna stitch in silver and oblong cross stitch in white wool, with just a slight touch of mauve metallized thread in tent stitch, completed the clasp. It is fastened with three small hooks and eyes.

Collars, cuffs and belts

When working a collar or small articles such as cuffs, belts and other costume ornaments, mark the outline of the shape required with a soft pencil, a fine paint brush or a felt-tipped pen upon the canvas. Cut the shape out with a border of approximately ¾ inch (2 cm.) of spare canvas all round. Fold this spare canvas over to the back of the work and, if necessary, baste it into position. Snip the edges of the canvas where required on curves. Oversew the two thicknesses of canvas around the edges to a depth of two to four threads, using yarn of an appropriate colour. When all the edges have been thus oversewn, it is an easy matter to complete the working of the design without danger of the canvas edges fraying.

It may sometimes be thought desirable to pad or raise part of the design, such as the edges of a collar (see page 118), above the rest of the work. To do this, lay string of a suitable thickness on the surface and stitch it down. If this is to be done along the edges of the canvas, it should be done before the oversewing is started. The oversewing stitches should be pulled tight and must cover the threads of the canvas completely.

The effect of a design can be lightened by cutting away certain areas of the canvas and this is done by starting from the centre of the area to be removed and cutting outwards to its outer edge. Cut any surplus canvas away leaving a narrow border, folding this to the back of the work. Oversew around the edges of the cut-out shape.

If beads, jewels or any 'found objects' are used in making these types of articles they must be firmly attached to the canvas either

These neck bands are attractive and quick to work in simple count-stitch patterns. The large black and bronze button used for the centre piece of the top band was the inspiration for the design, which is worked in bronze metallized thread and black silk. The two lower bands, which are unfinished, show clearly the method of working. △

130

An attractive bird and flower design which could be worked as a bedhead, as a long cushion or as a wall panel. Alternatively, a single bird shape could be taken from the design and used as a motif for a handbag or enlarged for a cushion. ▷

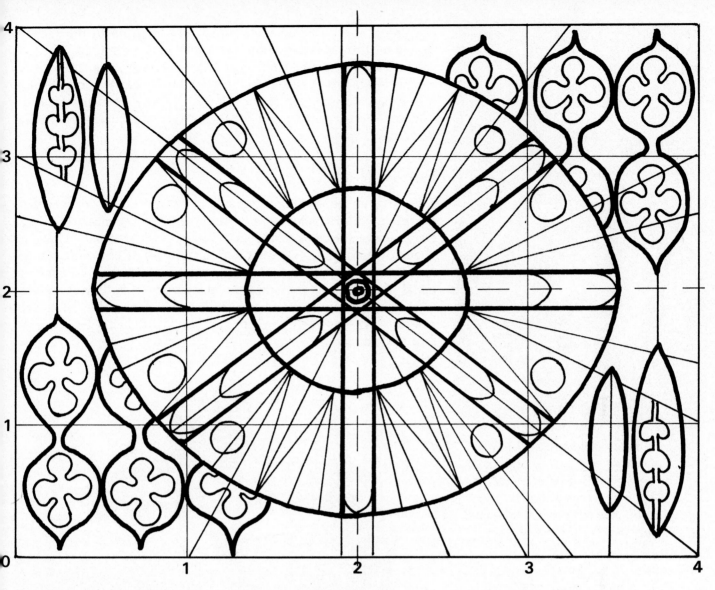

Stool-top design. Enlarge this diagram so that it measures 24 inches deep by 32 inches wide — or to the size of your stool-top. The colour scheme could be cool, using various shades of blue, dark purple, pink-mauves, shades of green and green-mustard. Alternatively, orange shades, burnt orange, reds, bright pink, petunia shades and a little lime yellow would look exciting. If the design appears complicated to a beginner, then only the darker lines could be worked and the remaining areas filled in using some of the attractive stitches in chapter 4. ▵

by gluing or by sewing them down. Fix them on to the canvas first, after the edges have been oversewn, and the stitchery is then worked around them. Care must be taken to see that no visible canvas is left unworked, something which can easily occur during this type of operation. There is nothing more irritating than to find one or two unworked stitches after the article has finally been made up.

Costume jewellery

The small metal shapes, obtainable in certain craft shops, which are intended for enamelling purposes, are ideal for mounting with canvas embroidery as pendants. If, however, a particular shape is needed which cannot be obtained in this way, it can probably be cut out of a tin can by using an old pair of kitchen scissors. A metal foundation is preferable to card, as it has sufficient weight to enable the pendant to hang well, and it is possible, after the canvas work has been glued to it, to bend the metal base to any required shape.

A small pendant, worked in emerald green coton perle and gold metallic thread, mounted upon a piece of metal cut from a tin can and covered with gold leather. The dimensions are 1¾ inches by 1¼ inches. △

A small pill-box hat worked on canvas is a novel idea. Gay colour and interesting stitches are all that are required for an attractive accessory. ▷

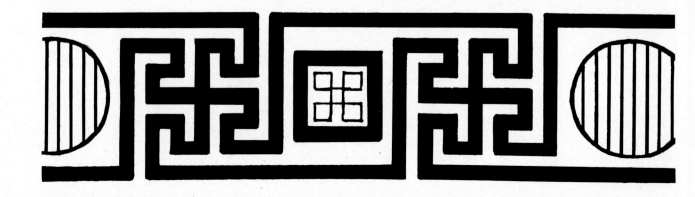

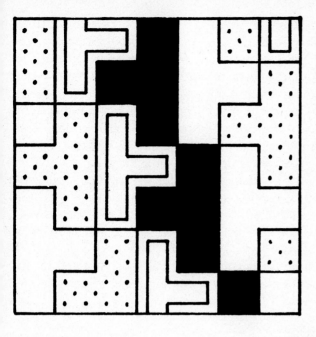

□ Any large flat stitch

■ Any large chunky stitch

▣ Outer edge, cross stitch; inner, flat stitch

⬚ Eyelets or bullion stitch

Some suggestions for abstract designs. All lines should be worked in tent stitch; other shapes and areas can be worked in some of the stitches given in the stitchery chapter. △

This geometric design may be enlarged to any size for working. The white crosses may be worked in french, bullion or norwich stitch, the black crosses in eyelets or gobelin stitch, the stripes in alternate lines of tent stitch in contrasting colours. ▷

This continuous design may be extended and enlarged to any size. Three or four colours will probably be sufficient. Work the black areas in gobelin or wheatsheaf stitch, the circles in long-legged cross or portuguese stem stitch, the background in italian two-sided, mosaic or tent stitch. ◁

133

Count stitch pattern, suitable for stool tops, cushions, handbags and many other objects. As indicated on the drawing, the stitch can be varied, perhaps using smyrna stitch within the design. ▽

If a bought metal shape is used for this work, trace the outline on to the canvas; this gives the area to be worked. After the embroidery has been completed, cut the spare canvas back to about four threads, and glue the piece of work firmly to the metal base. Fold the surplus canvas around the edges to the back and glue it down. Make two loops at the top, through which a suitable light chain can be threaded and this will ensure that the pendant will hang flat when worn. These loops can be made at the same time as the oversewing of the edges is done and with the same thread, or they can be fixed to the pendant during the making-up. A piece of gold or silver leather, ribbon or some silk material can be used for the backing, which is stitched carefully all round on to the canvas. Finish off the edges of the pendant with a fine silk .cord or a decorative edging of stitchery.

Metal bases intended for enamelling can also be obtained in the shape of rings. These can also have small pieces of canvas embroidery mounted upon them.

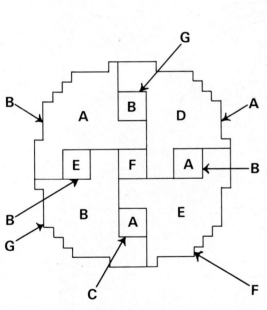

A light yellow

B medium yellow

C burnt yellow

D burnt orange

E greeny-blue

F medium blue

G emerald

CHOOSE SMALL STITCHES FOR BLACK SQUARES

A count stitch pattern △

8 Mounting finished work

Stretching the canvas

When a rectangular shaped piece of canvas embroidery has been completed and is removed from the frame, it may be discovered that the canvas has been pulled out of shape during the working. Although the canvas has been on a frame, this does sometimes happen and occurs particularly when tent stitch has been used extensively.

Before any attempt is made to mount a distorted piece of work, it must be pulled back into its original shape. To do this, stretch the work upon a drawing board which has first been covered with white cotton material or a sheet of white paper. Avoid brown paper for this purpose because it is liable to stain the work, if water has to be used to aid the process of stretching.

Place the embroidery face downwards upon the covered drawing board with one edge of the canvas in line with one edge of the board. This is done by first securing one corner of the canvas firmly in position with one or more drawing pins (thumb tacks) and then stretching the edge of the canvas taut until it reaches its correct length already marked on the edge of the board. Now fix the second corner of the canvas to the board and secure that whole side of the canvas down with drawing pins (thumb tacks) placed at intervals of half an inch to one inch. Mark the position of one of the other sides at right angles to the first on the drawing board and stretch the canvas taut along this line. Pin down the corner at the correct point and then put tacks along the whole side as before. To fix the other two sides correctly, their positions should be drawn in accurately on the background material and the fourth and last corner of the canvas should be fastened down by pulling the work taut and smoothing out any puckers until the corner is exactly in the position indicated and can be firmly fixed there. If this proves difficult to do, it may be necessary to sprinkle the back of the canvas with water, which should help to ease the worked material out to the required position. When the fourth corner is in position, the final two edges of the canvas can be stretched into place and fixed down as before.

Leave the work pinned on to the drawing board for twenty-four hours, by which time it will have dried out and can be safely removed.

A word of warning; when water is used to assist stretching, always avoid moistening an area where silk has been used in the working, because water penetrates silk much more readily that it does wool or cotton, and the surface of an area of silk may become water-stained. Also, if a canvas stiffened with size has been used, moisture may make the canvas limp and sticky. Only the minimum amount of water should be used on this type of canvas. To find out

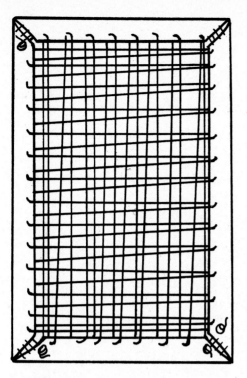

Diagram showing the method of mounting canvas work on to thick card or hardboard by lacing with strong thread.

if size has been used in the preparation of a certain piece of canvas, look at the mesh carefully to see if some of the holes have a slight covering of glue. It is the inexpensive type of canvas which is stiffened in this way.

For stretching pieces of canvas work other than rectangular panels, the method is more or less the same. The outline shape of articles such as stool-tops and chair seats should be clearly marked on the sheet of paper pinned to the drawing board and the finished piece of canvas work stretched and pinned down to fit the drawn shape as closely as possible. If, however, canvas work chair seats and backs and stool-tops are to be fitted to the furniture in question by a professional upholsterer, then leave the stretching of the canvas work to him.

Mounting wall panels

When a piece of canvas work intended for a picture or wall panel has been satisfactorily stretched, it should be mounted upon hard-board, after which it can be framed. Sometimes the work of mounting will be undertaken by a professional picture-framer but if there is any difficulty in getting this done satisfactorily, it is quite a simple procedure to carry out yourself. To mount on hard-board, first cut the hardboard to exactly the size of the worked area of the canvas, leaving about two inches of unworked canvas all round for attaching the work to the board. A strong adhesive such as Uhu, Copydex or Elmer's glue should be used, and the method of fixing is rather like that for stretching a worked canvas. Put a small amount of adhesive on the top edge of the board at one corner. Place the work in position on the board, and fold the un-worked canvas at the top over the edge and hold it firmly at the glued corner until it sticks. This will happen very quickly using one of the suggested adhesives. Apply the glue along the whole of the top edge of the board as far as the other corner. Pull the canvas taut and hold it firmly in position at this corner also until it has stuck. Fix the whole top edge of the canvas into position so that the embroidery comes right up to the edge of the mounting board, but not over it so that no unworked canvas shows on the front.

When this first side of the panel has been stuck down firmly in position along the edge of the board, stick the surplus canvas down on the back of the board. Attach a second side, one at right-angles to the first, to the board in a similar way, sticking the corners down first and then the side of the canvas between them. Fix the fourth corner and the final two sides in a similar way, after making sure that there is no sagging on the front of the work. Glue down the surplus unworked canvas on to the back of the board, and cut away any bulkiness at the corners.

Small panels of canvas work, which have kept their shape well during the working, may be attached to the hardboard backing simply by placing them in position and taking the unworked canvas over to the back of the board, where it is laced across from one side to the other with fine twine. It is important that the hard-board backing is cut large enough to allow the worked canvas to be stretched tight upon it, when it is laced up at the back, see diagram on this page.

A piece of canvas work has been mounted on to a wooden frame and fixed in position with tin-tacks. ▷

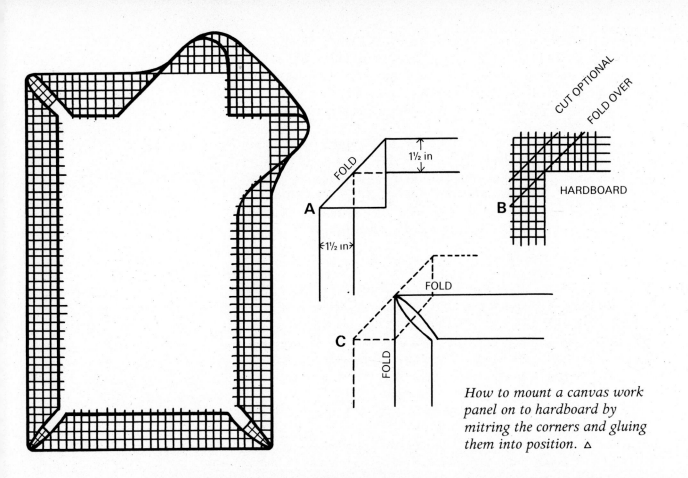

FOLD OVER

1½ in

FOLD

1½ in

A

B

HARDBOARD

FOLD

C

FOLD

How to mount a canvas work panel on to hardboard by mitring the corners and gluing them into position. △

Some workers may choose to mount a canvas work panel upon a strong piece of ply-wood (five-ply is the most suitable thickness). The panel is fixed in position by placing gimp or braid-pins through the canvas along the outer edges of the board at intervals of about half an inch, while lacing the surplus canvas neatly across the back.

If a canvas work panel is very large and heavy, it may need to be mounted on a strong wooden frame instead of upon hardboard or ply-wood. Stretch the canvas over the frame and fix it with $\frac{3}{8}$ inch tacks at intervals of approximately $\frac{1}{2}$ inch all round the outer edge of the frame. A pair of upholsterer's stretchers may be needed to stretch the last two sides of the canvas into position.

Framing

The panel is now ready to be framed. Canvas work panels are much improved if a mount covered with coarse linen is placed between the panel and the outer frame. This has the effect of isolating the embroidery from its immediate surroundings thus giving it importance. The choice of colour for this mount is important, for, although in most cases a neutral shade may seem most suitable, the appearance of a piece of canvas embroidery is often greatly enhanced by the skilful choice of a rather brighter colour.

A final important point to remember is that all canvas work should be framed without glass if it is to be seen to best effect. If the framing is being done professionally, this point needs to be stressed to the framer at the start. The use of glass, when framing this sort of work, makes it very difficult to observe the full effect of the embroidery. Reflections on the glass tend to obscure textural effects of the stitchery, and, as wool, which is used very considerably in canvas work, always retains a certain amount of moisture, sweating and misting-up of the glass will occur, if the panel is hung where it may become heated by the warmth from a radiator or from sunlight. Non-reflective glass, recommended by some picture-framers, should also be avoided at all costs. It has a dreadful distorting effect and gives the embroidery the appearance of an oleograph.

Mounting mirror surrounds

When mounting canvas work surrounds for mirrors, you can easily complete the work of mounting for yourself by following a few simple instructions. The glass for the mirror can be either bevelled or unbevelled, but the use of bevelled glass is to be recommended, as it ensures a first-class result, although the work will take longer to complete than if unbevelled glass were used.

The bevelled glass should be slightly larger all round than the aperture in the canvas work surround. Place the glass centrally upon a piece of half-inch thick hardboard or ply-wood, which will form the base and should have the same outside measurements as the worked surround. Build up this baseboard all round the mirror to the thickness of the glass by gluing lengths of strong card, ply-wood or hardboard to it. In addition to forming a level ground to take the embroidery surround the strips will also help to hold the mirror in position. Mount the embroidery upon a piece of thin hardboard which has been cut to its exact shape and size and has,

138

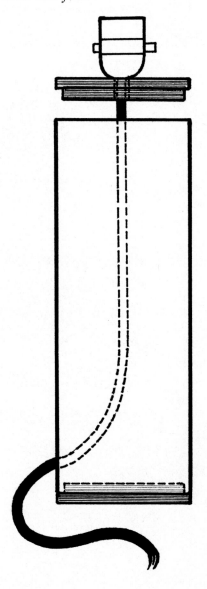

Diagram showing the method for fitting the tube with lamp holder and flex.

therefore, an aperture which is slightly smaller than the mirror. After carrying the inner and outer edges of the canvas over the edges of the mount, glue them down carefully and firmly on the wrong side, place the mounted surround in position on the mirror and glue it down. The mirror will now be held firmly in place and the whole thing is ready for framing. If the embroidery is very elaborate, and jewels have been used in the working, a narrow, fairly plain frame is all that will be required.

For mounting a mirror of unbevelled glass, it is necessary to have the glass cut to the same size as the hardboard base, fixing it in position with mirror clips. The mounted canvas work surround is then placed in position on top of the glass, and the whole thing is framed.

All canvas work placed upon a mirror made of heavy plate glass must have the inner edge next to the mirror lined in some way, as this type of glass gives a deep reflection.

Either work a few extra lines of stitchery all round the centre aperture to mask the thickness of the hardboard mount and to prevent the bare, unworked canvas being reflected in the glass, or, if preferred, a suitable narrow braid can be glued on to the inner edge of the surround before it is finally placed in position on the mirror.

Table lamp bases

Attractive table lamp bases can be made by working a rectangular shape on canvas, which is then wrapped around and attached to a length of asbestos or plastic piping (the type of piping used by builders for boiler chimneys). Alternatively, the canvas can be applied to a piece of thick cardboard tubing.

It is best to acquire a suitable piece of piping or cardboard tubing before the design is made and worked, as careful measurements must be taken to decide the height and width of the canvas work needed to cover the base adequately. The stove pipes come in varying sizes, but a diameter of $4\frac{1}{2}$ to $5\frac{1}{2}$ inches is best for the purpose, and a popular length is twelve to fourteen inches. From a builders' supplier a three-foot length of asbestos piping can be obtained, but it usually has a collar at one end which is intended for joining the pipes together, and this has first to be removed by cutting the pipe with a hack-saw. One is then left with enough piping for two or three lamp bases. Sometimes it is possible to get a broken pipe from a builder, and this can be cut down to the right size.

If a plastic pipe or cardboard tube is used to make a lamp base, this will probably have to be weighted to enable it to stand firmly, and a plastic bag filled with sand, placed inside the tube, will achieve this. It is possible to cut this type of pipe with a hack-saw in the same way as for the asbestos piping, smoothing it off with sandpaper afterwards. When the tube for the table lamp has been selected and cut to the length required, drill a hole in the side about one inch up from the base and large enough to allow the electric flex for the lamp to pass through. Draw a pencil line vertically down the side of the lamp base tube, so that it passes through the point where the flex comes out. This line is to assist in placing the worked canvas accurately in position for fixing. Cover the open ends of the tube with circular wooden covers cut from seven-ply

Cardboard and asbestos tubes for making up table lamp bases, together with circular wooden covers for fitting into the ends of the tubes.

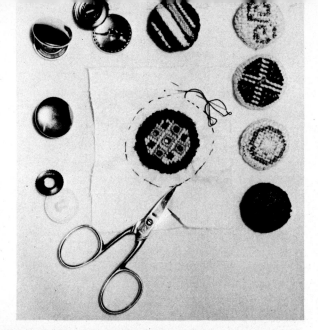

To mount canvas work on metal button moulds, cut surrounding canvas back to the edge of the embroidery. Place the work on a piece of fine cotton material and stitch it down all round with the background wool, so that any bare canvas is covered. Outline the embroidery with gathering stitches, working about ¼ inch away from the edges. Cut the surplus fabric away. Pull the gathering up to fit the button mount and finish off the button to manufacturers' instructions.

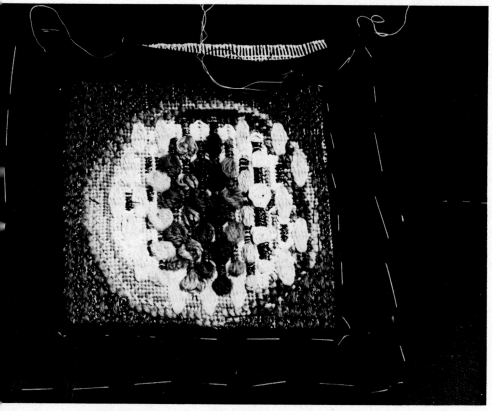

This is a six-inch square of canvas work on 14 mesh canvas in the process of being mounted on furnishing fabric. This is an excellent way of making attractive cushions, which involve very little work. The raw edge of the furnishing fabric is covered in this instance with ric-rac braid, which fits in very well with the hungarian stitch background.

wood to the same diameter as the outer surface of the tube, so that the covers fit exactly over the open ends of the tube. Cut two smaller circular pieces of ply-wood, this time to fit into the opening at each end, and glue them firmly to the centre of each of the larger pieces, so that the wooden covers fit into the ends of the tube like stoppers. Drill a hole through the centre of the top cover and fix a lamp holder in position over the hole. When the flex has been passed through the lamp base and attached to the lamp holder, the wooden covers at each end are glued firmly into position.

(If difficulty is experienced in making the circular wooden covers for a table lamp base, small wooden base boards, which are used for basket-making, can be bought and used instead. These basket bases have small holes bored all round them, but they can

140

A rectangle of canvas embroidery is set into a surround of furnishing material. The design was inspired by the piano keyboard. ▷

easily be covered with leather or canvas work during the making-up.)

Work the piece of embroidery and cut the unworked canvas away to leave a half-inch border all round. This border is carefully turned under the work along the top and bottom edges and down one of the sides, but on the other side it is used to attach the work to the tube. Place the last line of stitchery exactly on the vertical line drawn upon the tube and glue the strip of unworked canvas beside it on to the tube. When the canvas has been securely stuck down, pull the embroidery firmly round the tube until the two sides meet and stitch them edge to edge.

The way in which the circular wooden covers at top and bottom of the tube are finished off will depend upon whether or not the piece of canvas embroidery has been worked deep enough to cover their edges as well as the outer surface of the tube. If this is so, the top can be covered either with leather or a piece of fabric, whilst the underside of the base should have a covering of baize or felt. If, however, the edges of the wooden covers are to remain visible after the embroidery has been applied, a good effect may be achieved by staining and varnishing both top and bottom covers. Alternatively, the top can be covered with leather or fabric and a simple braid or a plait of wool can be fixed around both top and bottom edges. The underside of the base should be covered as before with baize or felt.

Table lamp bases may also require a template or pattern for the design. The height of this will be the height of the piece of tube chosen for the base, plus the thickness of the top and bottom wooden covers for the tube, if it is intended to cover these with embroidery, and the width will be the circumference of the tube, plus an extra quarter of an inch which is allowed for the thickness of the wool used in the work.

A chair squab with its new needlework cover tacked in position. The corners have been mitred, and the raw edges of the canvas turned under. It is now ready for its final covering of hessian, which will be stretched right over the base of the squab and tacked down.

Index